WHAT PEOPLE ARE ~~~~~...

Actuarial humour is like a dog walking on his hind legs.
It is not well done, but you are surprised to find it done at all.

Dr Samuel Johnson (adapted)

The problem with actuarial jokes is not the jokes themselves, but that if you get them, you don't have any friends to tell them to.

You know how awful the average actuarial joke is?
Well, by definition, half of them are even worse than that.

J.R. "Bob" Dobbs (adapted)

THE ULTIMATE

ACTUARIAL

JOKE BOOK

OTHER BOOKS BY THE AUTHOR

Actuarial/mathematical/Excel
memes & jokes

www.actuarialtutor.substack.com

THE ULTIMATE

ACTUARIAL

JOKE BOOK

670.5 jokes geeky enough
to be suitable for actuaries

JOHN LEE

The Ultimate Actuarial Joke Book: 670.5 Jokes Geeky Enough to be Suitable for Actuaries

Published by:

Kingdom Collective Publishing

KCP

Unit 10936, PO Box 6945

London, W1A 6US

kingdomcollectivepublishing@gmail.com

Book and Cover idea by John Lee, design by 100covers
ISBN: 978-1-912045-11-2

First Edition: July 2022

DEDICATION

This book is dedicated to those rare actuaries whose sense of humour survived the actuarial qualification process.

Albeit irreparably damaged beyond all recognition, but survived nonetheless.

ACKNOWLEDGEMENTS

I am once again indebted to my beta readers, who undertook the gruelling task of exposing themselves to 100 jokes a week for 10 weeks to ensure I kept only the very best.

However, I had not anticipated the effect sustained exposure to actuarial jokes would have on my reviewers dropping out, as their Kaplan-Meier survival function reveals:

Week	S(t)
1	0.833
2	0.667
3	0.583
4	0.500
7	0.333
10	0.167

So many, many thanks to Greg Solomon, Jordan Chong, Adam Biros, Musaddiqe Ahmed, Oliver Scanlon, Kanishka Singhal, Emma Wang, Leigh Costanza, Mary Pat Campbell, David Yardley and Shaikh Mujtaba Ali.

CONTENTS

RISK MANAGEMENT

Every effort has been taken to ensure these jokes are bland enough to be suitable for actuaries. However, due to my small reviewer sample size and the fact that some of my reviewers were only *part* qualified, there is a small, but statistically significant, probability that funny jokes remain.

Since laughter is behaviour unbecoming of any serious actuary and may result in breaching the Actuaries' Code of Conduct, I recommend you take appropriate risk mitigation measures, such as:

- Subcontracting the reading of this book, and its accompanying risks, to a non-actuary.

- Reducing the rate of humour intake by reading slowly and squinting.

- Reading the book in a cold and draughty location to ensure high levels of alertness for possible funniness.

- Thinking morbid thoughts to maintain a sober mind-set.

- Pinching yourself whenever necessary so that the pain will distract you from the urge to laugh.

- Make liberal use of the spreadsheet safe space overleaf.

SPREADSHEET SAFE SPACE

Please find below a complimentary image of a spreadsheet to refer to whenever you find yourself threatened by humour or attempted humour within the pages of this book.

WHAT IS AN ACTUARY?

An actuary is a device for turning coffee into spreadsheets.

Paul Erdos (adapted)

DEFINITIONS

An actuary is a professional who diligently collects data, analyses it and then draws confusions.

An actuary is somebody who expects everyone to be dead on time.

Actuary: a place where they bury dead actors.

An actuary is an expert who can solve a problem you didn't even know you had in a way you can't understand.

An actuary is a person whose lifetime ambition is to be wrong at most 5% of the time.

An actuary is someone who insists on being certain about uncertainty.

WHAT'S THE DIFFERENCE?

What's the difference between an actuary and a zombie?
Zombies lose their personality *after* dying.[1]

What's the difference between an actuary and a fungus?
A fungus can grow on you.

What's the difference between a sperm and an actuary?
The sperm has a one in ten million chance of becoming a
human being.

What's the difference between an actuary and a mortician?
Nobody's dying to see an actuary.

What's the difference between an actuary and a lawyer?
The actuary knows they are boring.

---

[1] Kanishka Singhal.

What's the difference between an actuary and a terrorist?

You can negotiate with a terrorist.

What's the difference between an actuary and a plant?

A plant has a better social life.[2]

What's the difference between an actuary and a corpse?

The corpse is better dressed.

---

[2] Kanishka Singhal.

YOU MIGHT BE AN ACTUARY IF...

You flinch when anybody says the word exam.

Somebody asks the rhetorical question "What are the odds?"
and you know the answer.

All the money in your wallet
faces the same direction.

You believe a "half-day" means leaving at 5 pm.

Going on holiday
means getting 20 hours of CPD.

You feel the uncontrollable urge to explain your jokes.

You believe that the perfect anniversary present for your
spouse is additional life insurance on yourself.

You require PowerPoint to explain what you do for a living.

You decide which pizza is better value
by calculating the price per area.

You write memos in Excel.

The office motion sensor lights often switch off
when you're working.

ACTUARIAL QUALIFICATIONS

FIA

~~Fellow of the Institute of Actuaries (UK)~~

Finger in Air

FFA

~~Fellow of the Faculty of Actuaries (Scotland)~~

Friends and Family Abandoned

FSA

~~Fellow of the Society of Actuaries (US)~~

Forget Social Activities

FCAS

~~Fellow of the Casualty Actuarial Society (US)~~

F***ing Clever At Sums

BUMPER STICKERS[3]

Actuaries do it until disability, death or withdrawal.

Actuaries do it discretely but continuously.

Actuaries do it on random walks.

Insurance agents do it with third parties.

Statisticians do it with only a 5% chance of being rejected.

Actuaries do it with 95% confidence.

Actuaries do it with varying rates of interest.

Bayesian actuaries do it with a posterior.

---

[3] For those unfamiliar with this joke structure, the "it" is a double entendre having two interpretations – one being what actuaries do in their job, the other is risqué.

OLD ACTUARIES

Old actuaries never die...

they just get broken down by age and sex[4].

Old actuaries never die...

they are simply seasonally adjusted.

Old actuaries never die...

they just become non-significant.

Old insurance actuaries never retire...

they just expire.

Old mathematicians never die...

they just lose some of their functions.

---

[4] Attributed to Bob Crompton.

UNUSUAL ACTUARIES

Why did the actuarial vampire get fired?
Because she was afraid of the stakeholders.[5]

What is the difference between an English actuary
and a Sicilian actuary?
An English actuary can tell you how many people are going to
die next year.
The Sicilian actuary can tell you whom and their addresses.[6]

The statistician realised that he almost certainly has prostate
issues.
Because his pee value was really small.

I'm terrified of numbers that aren't the ratio of two integers.
It's really irrational.

---

[5] A John Lee original.

[6] If you're confused, it's because you haven't realised that the Mafia are Sicilian.

Why did the actuary lose their faith in humanity?
They realised that the average person is also the meanest.

What do you get when you cross a pirate with a data scientist?
Someone who specialises in Rrrr.

A Bayesian actuary is someone who, vaguely expecting a horse, and catching a glimpse of a donkey, strongly believes he has seen a mule.[7]

Did you hear about the actuary who couldn't afford lunch?
She could binomial.[8]

What do you call an actuary with a sense of humour?
An outlier.[9]

Did you hear about the actuary who plotted his name?
It was his auto*graph*.

---

[7] Attributed to Dr Charles Annis.

[8] Buy-no-meal.

[9] John Lee, but probably not original.

Did you hear about the actuary who lost control?

Fortunately, the IT department gave them a new keyboard.

Did you hear about the actuary who was given a pet lamb?

She called it "Da".

It was her λ.[10]

What did the actuarial Jedi say?

May the force of interest be with you.[11]

---

[10] John Lee, but probably not original.

[11] John Lee, but probably not original.

PERSONALITY

The reason that every major
university maintains a department
of mathematics is that
it's cheaper to do this than to
institutionalise all those people.

BORING/DULL?

What do you call a plane full of actuaries?
A Boring 747.

Why did the actuarial pig never go to parties?
He was a boar.[12]

Have you heard the one about the fun/interesting actuary?
No, me neither.

People only call actuaries boring until they learn how much
money they make.
Then they call them rich and boring.[13]

What do you call an actuary with a sense of humour?
Part Qualified.

---

[12] John Lee, because who else could come up with a joke this bad...?

[13] John Lee

People think actuaries are dull but I'll have you know that the H in actuary stands for hip.[14]

What happens when you put a wild hyena in the same room as an actuary?

The hyena stops laughing.

An actuary was explaining to her psychiatrist how everyone in the world thinks she's boring.

"Nonsense," replies the psychiatrist,

"Not everyone in the world knows you."

Did you hear about the terrorists who hijacked a plane full of actuaries?

They threatened to release one each hour until their demands were met.

How do you make an actuary laugh on Monday?

Tell them a joke on Friday.

---

[14] John Lee. If you're thinking "but there's no H in actuary!" you have missed the whole point of the joke.

I got called pretty today.

Actually, the full sentence was,

"You're a pretty boring actuary."

But I'm focussing on the positive.

What is the most radical thing an actuary does?

Calculate square roots.

What do actuaries do to liven up the office party?

Not show up.

When does someone decide to pursue an actuarial career?

When they realise they lack the charisma required to be a

successful undertaker.

When do actuaries laugh out loud?

When somebody asks them to be certain.

Psychologist to actuary: The problem is that you're boring.

Actuary: I'd like a second opinion, please.

Psychologist: OK, you're ugly as well.[15]

---

[15] John Lee, but probably not original.

SHY

What do you call an actuary who speaks to one person a day?
Popular.

One actuary was so scared of being in an elevator in close proximity to other people that she took steps to avoid them.

Did you hear about the particularly shy actuary?
He ran out of sick days to avoid client meetings
and so ended up calling in dead.

Did you hear about the statistician who went through
Dale Carnegie training?
She improved her confidence from 95% to 99%.

How can you spot an extroverted actuary at a party?
He's the one staring at someone else's shoes.[16]

---

[16] Attributed to Al Beer.

Actuaries are sick of the pandemic and the 2 metre distancing. They're looking forward until it's over when they can go back to their usual 15 meter distancing.[17]

How did the actuary ensure that no-one talked to her whilst on holiday?
She wore a sign saying:
"Insurance agent. Ask about our term-life insurance package."

What do UFOs and shy actuaries have in common?
You hear about them all the time,
but you never actually see one.

When they simultaneously spot a $100 bill while out strolling, Santa Claus, the tooth fairy, an outgoing actuary, and an elderly drunken man stop in their tracks.
Who is the lucky one who gets it?
The old drunk, obviously.
The other three are mythological beings.

---

[17] John Lee

THOROUGH OR OCD?

Why do old actuaries get upset when people say
"age is just a number"?
Because age is a word, not a number!

The actuaries' prayer:
Lord, help me be less stressed about insignificant details,
starting tomorrow at 09.14:15 am
British Summer Time.

What's the best way to drive an actuary totally crazy?
Tie them up, and force them to watch you
fold up a road map incorrectly.

Where do you bury actuaries with OCD?
A symmetry.

How do you keep an actuary in the shower for the entire day?
Give them a bottle of shampoo which says:
"lather, rinse and repeat."

Did you hear about the actuary who was afraid
of negative numbers?
She stopped at nothing to avoid them.

My family is worried about my addiction to
performing graduation by hand.
It's OK; I know where to draw the line.[18]

Why did the actuary hate obtuse angles?
Because they just weren't right.

Yesterday, I asked an actuary to go to the back of the queue.
He came back five minutes later and explained that he
couldn't as someone else was already there.

---

[18] John Lee

The optimist thinks the glass is half full.

The pessimist thinks the glass is half empty.

The actuary thinks the glass is twice the size it needs to be.

As an actuary, I often wonder if I analyse things too much...

...or maybe not enough?

An actuary is having trouble sleeping and visits her doctor. "Have you ever tried to count sheep?" the doctor asks.

"That's the issue. I don't know how many there were last quarter, nor if all the sheep are reported.

Also, I have to apply a survivorship factor as I don't know if earlier sheep will still be alive by the time the count is finished. Then I find I've made an error and so spend two hours looking for it..."

Three men are to be executed by guillotine. As soon as the first man steps up and inserts his head into the hole, the executioner releases the knife. Miraculously, the blade stops just millimetres above the man's neck. The king declares, "In accordance with our nation's laws, if the guillotine fails, you are free."

The first man walks free whilst the second places his head into the hole. Again, the guillotine blade stops millimetres above the man's neck. The king declares again, "In accordance with our nation's laws, if the guillotine fails, you are free." So the second man goes free.

The third man, an actuary, looks up as he inserts his head into the guillotine hole and says, "I believe I've discovered what the problem is..."

A report published today shows that 4/10 children
are living in poverty.
I think that is disgusting and is indicative of all
that is wrong in this country.
That fraction should have been simplified to 2/5.

People complain that I make far too many assumptions.
I mean, they don't actually come out and say it,
but I know that's exactly what they're thinking...

A farmer and an actuary were taking the train together.

"There are 1,236 sheep out there," observed the actuary as they passed a flock of sheep in a meadow.

"Amazing," the farmer replied. "By chance, I happen to know the owner, and that number is exactly right.

How were you able to count them so fast?"

The actuary answered,

"It was easy. I simply counted the number of legs and divided the total by four."

LOGICAL OR EMOTIONALLY STUNTED?

Why didn't the actuary like pie?
Because she was rational.

I used to feel like I was just a statistic, but the psychiatrist
diagnosed me with multiple personality disorder.
Now I feel like a distribution.

An actuary was asked about the meaning of life.
They replied: "It depends on the parameter values."

An actuary's wife delivers a baby,
which is handed to the actuary.
"Is it a boy or a girl?" she asks.
"Yes," he replied actuarially.

Why are actuaries like tennis players?
Love means nothing to them.

The doctor visits his heart transplant patient.

"I've got great news! Two donors available from whom we can choose your new heart."

The patient is delighted and asks, "Who did they belong to?"

"The first was the heart of a 26-year-old marathon runner, and the second was the heart of a 55-year-old actuary."

"I'll take the actuary's heart," declares the patient.

"I'd like one that's never been used."

Of course, actuaries are flexible!

Either they are correct or they can prove it to be so.

GEEKY AKA COOL ACTUARIES

How does an actuary become more trendy?

She applies a moving average to her life.[19]

Why do actuaries travel in groups of 2 or 4?

So they don't appear odd.

What's an actuary's idea of trashing a hotel room?

Refusing to complete the guest comment card.

What do you call a group of male actuaries

who love equations?

Alge-bros.

What do π and actuaries talking about Excel have in

common?

They both go on forever.[20]

---

[19] John Lee

[20] John Lee

How do actuaries say goodbye?

Calc-u-later.

Why do actuaries have great abs?

Because they're good at number crunching.

Actuaries think good health is just the slowest rate at which
you can die.

People call us stats geeks, yet the truth is that we're actually
sum of the least squares.

Who's in favour of reintroducing Roman numerals?

I for one.

Why are actuaries like hipsters?

They did maths before it became cool. Hold up, that hasn't
happened yet. But one day they will be like hipsters. Honest.[21]

---

[21] John Lee

What's an actuary's favourite chocolate selection?

Qualitative Street.[22]

In Canada, there's a group that refuses to speak English.

They're called separatists and typically live in Quebec.

In America, they're called actuaries.

Have you heard about the actuary who worked out too much?

They were overfit.[23]

A group of actuaries in the same office had heard the same jokes so many times that they assigned them numbers. Instead of telling the entire joke, they would simply shout out its number, to save time.

""8," shouted one of them. The other actuaries laughed loudly at this old classic.

"136," shouted another one. Most of the other actuaries laughed mildly, except for a new actuary to the department, who was rolling around the floor laughing hysterically.

---

[22] Quality Street is a British chocolate selection box.

[23] Jordan Goldmeier

One of the others asked, "What is it about joke 136 that makes it so darn hilarious?"

"I'd never heard that joke before!"

Another time, after a few jokes had been told, one actuary shouted, "285!" No-one laughed, and a few actuaries scowled at him.

The actuary leaned over to one of the other actuaries and asked what was wrong.

"Young man, we don't tell dirty jokes when ladies are present."

One day, an actuary new to the office, says "74."

Nobody laughs. He tries again with "32." Not even a smile.

Then some of the other actuaries shouted numbers, and they all laughed again.

The new actuary asked another actuary, "Why didn't anyone laugh at my joke?" The other actuary replies, "It's all in how you tell them."

SENSIBLE OR RISK AVERSE?

Why did the actuary want to be buried in Jerusalem?
Higher rate of resurrection.

Did you hear about the actuary who took up jogging after he
heard it would add years to his life?
It worked – he feels 10 years older already.

My father told me I should begin reciting statistics
if anyone ever threatens me with a gun.
Apparently, there's safety in numbers.

Why don't vegan actuaries take risks?
Because their life could be at steak.

There was this actuary on a bus throwing bits of torn
newspaper out the window.
One passenger asked, "What are you doing?"
The actuary replied, "Keeping the elephants away."
"What elephants?" asked the passenger incredulously.
"Good, isn't it?" replied the actuary.

An actuary, when driving her car, would always accelerate quickly before every intersection, zip right through it, and then immediately slow down once she'd passed it.

One day, she took a passenger, who was understandably unnerved by her driving style, and asked her why she went so fast over intersections. The actuary replied, "Well, statistically, you're significantly more likely to have an accident at an intersection, so I accelerate to reduce the time spent there."

An actuary gets on a plane. The guy next to him says "I'm scared of flying." The actuary says "I used to be, as I was scared of terrorists blowing up the plane." "How did you overcome your fear?" asked the guy. The actuary replied "I now bring a bomb onto the plane." The now terrified man screams, "What!?"

The actuary replies, "Calm down. I'm not going to blow myself up, but the odds that there are two bombs on one plane are now almost insignificant." [24]

---

[24] However, the actuary failed to account for independent events and the explosion was twice as big.

ACTUARIAL THOUGHTS

Does Auld Lang Syne imply the existence of
Auld Lang Cosyne and Auld Lang Tangynt?

What's the single form of calcul*us*?
Calcul*me* or calcul*i*.

Which phrase is correct:
"All prime numbers are odd except one"
or "All prime numbers are odd except two"?

Are prime numbers like people who smoke weed?
As the higher they are, the more spaced out they get.

Are the last few available graves in a cemetery called
residual plots?

ACTUARIES IN THE OUTSIDE WORLD

Why don't actuaries like to model new clothes?

Lack of fit.

Doctor: "I'm afraid you have type I diabetes."

Actuary: "That's a relief. I thought I had diabetes."[25]

Why did the actuary spill all her food in the oven?

Because the cooking instructions said,

"Place it in the oven at 180 degrees."

I called a local restaurant the other night and asked,

"Do you do takeaways?"

They said "Yes," so I asked,

"What's 26,138 minus 475?"

---

[25] The actuary is confusing type I diabetes with a type 1 error where a true hypothesis (in this case, that they have diabetes) is rejected.

What's a polar bear?

A Cartesian bear in a different co-ordinate system.

Judge to actuary: "I sentence you to life or 100 years."

Actuary to judge: "Can I have life as it's statistically shorter?"

Why do actuaries always book a table before going to a restaurant? Because they know the importance of reserving.[26]

How do actuaries like their steak?

Median rare.

---

[26] John Lee

An actuary goes to the store for a loaf of bread. As he leaves his wife says, "And if they have eggs, buy a dozen." So the actuary comes home with a dozen loaves of bread.

Why shouldn't you share your food with an actuary? Because they always want a large sample.

A man in a hot-air balloon realises that he's lost. He sees someone on the ground and shouts out, "Excuse me, could you let me know where I am?" The woman on the ground thinks for a moment and replies, "you are exactly 22.48 metres above this spot on the ground."

The man is balloon says, "You must be an actuary."

"I am. How did you know?" she replies.

"You gave me information that is totally correct but completely useless."

The actuary responds, "Well, you must be in marketing."

The man in the balloon replies, "I am. How did you know?"

"Because you're exactly in the same position as before but now it's my fault."[27]

---

[27] Attributed to Fred Kilbourne improved upon by both John Dinius and Stacey Haws.

BAD ACTUARIES

How can you tell that you're in the hands of
the Actuarial Mafia?
They make you an offer that you can't understand.

Did you hear about the actuary who was thrown in jail?
His degrees of freedom reduced significantly.

After enough alcohol all statisticians
tend to become Bayesians.
They start making inferences from their posterior.

What do you call an actuary who never tells the truth?
A straight outlier.

Have you heard about the actuary who was so negative?
People would look around when she walked into a room
and say, "Who just left?"

I got arrested the other day for vandalising
the axioms of mathematics.
I got let off, though. Nothing could be proved.

An arrogant actuary was prescribed anti-gloating cream,
but he's still rubbing it in.

What do you call a sudden urge to solve differential equations?
Calculust.

My actuarial colleague and I laugh about how competitive we
are.
But I laugh more.

Did you hear about the South African actuary?
She was addicted to meth.

Many people say actuaries like me are egocentric,
but enough about them.[28].

---

[28] John Lee, but probably not original.

Why should you worry if you see an actuary with graph paper?
Because they're plotting something.

I got pulled over while doing calculus in my car last night.
The cop said I was deriving over the limit.

What risk is the Actuaries' Code of Conduct exposed to?
Moral hazard.[29]

I knew an actuary who always wore a stethoscope
around his neck.
So in emergencies, he'd teach people an
important lesson about making assumptions.

Why do actuaries always go back to being cruel?
Reversion to the mean.[30]

---

[29] John Lee

[30] John Lee

I picked up a hitchhiker the other night on the way home
from work.

He said, "Aren't you worried I'm might have been a murderer
or something?"

I said, "What are the chances of there being *two* murderers
in the same car at the same time?

RELATIONSHIPS

Statistics is like a man. With a bit of manipulation, you can get out of it what you want.

Yvette Konijnenberg

STARTING OUT

An actuary introduces himself to a pretty lady in a bar.

"Hi, I'm an actuary, what do you do?"

"I'm a model," she replied.

The actuary replies excitedly, "That's so cool!

What are your assumptions?"[31]

I asked a gorgeous statistician for her phone number.

She replied, "Probably not."

I just met a girl named Ellen.

She's the complete inverse of my e^x.[32]

Did you hear about the actuary's girlfriend?

She was $\sqrt{-100}$.

A perfect 10, but purely imaginary.

---

[31] John Lee

[32] Ellen sounds like "ln" which is short for natural log, the opposite of e^x.

Did you hear about the actuary that had been out with a
number of girls?

Zero was the number.

Two actuaries are coming out of work. As the first actuary was
opening his car door, he notices the other getting on a bike.
"What's with the new bike?"

The second actuary says, "Yeah, the strangest thing happened
to me yesterday. A woman rode up to me on this bike. She
threw the bike to the ground, ripped off all her clothes and
yelled, 'TAKE WHAT YOU WANT.' So I decided to take the
bike.

The first actuary nods approvingly, "Good choice. The clothes
probably wouldn't have fit."

Did you hear about the actuary who wrote to
the lonely hearts club?

They wrote back saying that they just weren't that lonely.

Did you hear about the actuary who was asked out by 20 girls?

He accidentally went into the girls' shower room.

How does an actuary get a date?

Work in Excel, you'll be given one when you least expect it.[33]

Last night, while I was browsing an Excel blog, an ad popped up for hot singles in my area who want to HLOOKUP[34].

What did the middle-aged actuary use as a chat-up line to the new girl in the office?

"You're the type of girl I could take home to my mother, which is just as well, because I'm still living with her."

I asked a statistician out on a date.

She failed to reject me.

---

[33] John Lee

[34] Or perhaps it should be VHOOKUP?

PICK UP LINES

What's an actuary's favourite one-liner?

$y = mx + c$.

From the first time I saw you, my interest
in you has compounded continuously.

My affection for you is a monotonic increasing
function of time.

Are you a related data set in a separate table?
Because I INDEX/MATCH you.

Are you a deferred asset?
Because I see some long-term benefits in you.

I model for a living.

FIRST DATES

This really hot chick in my apartment complex told me she
wants us to be "friends with benefits".
Does anyone know where I can purchase a group
health insurance plan?

The woman said she was approaching 40,
but the actuary wondered from what direction.

I went out to dinner with an actuary who was
obsessed with addition.
I've never seen so many positive signs on a first date.

What do women and unit-linked insurance policies have in
common?
Both are hard to understand, costly
and what you get is not guaranteed.

What's the difference between men and endowment policies?
An endowment policy eventually matures.

My girlfriend was mad at me, so she started talking in binary.
I was like, "Well! 10 can play at that game!"

Girl: Tell me 3 words that are better than I love you!
Actuarial student: independent identically distributed.

During our last date night, I leaned over to my girlfriend and
whispered: "null, nada, nil, naught, zilch, zero."
She loves it when I whisper sweet nothings in her ear.

My ex said we split up because I rely too much on logic and
refuse to acknowledge my feelings.
I replied, "Correlation is not causation."

Two women are chatting. "How did your blind date
with that actuary go?" asked the first.
"I had to slap him!" the second replies
"Did he try it on?"
"No. I was worried he was dead!"

Actuaries love the person they spend the most time with.
As that's their statistically significant other.

An actuary went on a date, and the following day her colleague
asks how it went.
"Not too good. I just couldn't stop myself from talking about
how much I love simplifying fractions."
"Yeah, you really shouldn't have mentioned mathematics on
the first date."
"Well, you know the saying. Hindsight is 1."[35]

My girlfriend let me know on Valentine's Day
that our romance was not a "going concern".

Why are actuaries such players?
Because they're up all night with different models.

---

[35] The common idiom is "hindsight is 50:50"

After a thorough physical examination, a patient arrived at her doctor's office.

"I've got some dreadful news for you," said the doctor, "I'm afraid you've only got five months left to live."

The patient gasped, "What should I do?"

The doctor answered, "I suggest you find an actuary and marry them."

"Will that help me live much longer?"

"No, but it will *feel* like it."

I constructed a graph of all my past relationships.

It has an ex-axis and a why-axis.

A man was crossing a road when he heard a frog say, "If you kiss me, I'll turn into a beautiful princess." He knelt, scooped up the frog, and placed it in his pocket.

From the pocket, the frog said, "If you kiss me and turn me into a princess, I'll tell everyone how clever and brave you are." The man pulled the frog out, smiled at it, and put it right back.

The frog added, "If you kiss me and turn me into a princess, I'll also be your girlfriend for a week." The man pulled the frog out again, smiled at it, and put it right back.

From the pocket, the frog pleaded, "If you kiss me and turn me into a princess, I'll marry you, and cook all your meals, and wash your laundry." Once more, the man took out the frog, smiled at it, and put it right back.

Finally, the frog begged, "What's the problem? I've told you I'm a princess and that I'll marry you and cook your meals and even wash your laundry. Why do you refuse to kiss me?"

"Look, I'm an actuary," the man replied, "So, I simply have no time for a wife. However I have to admit, a talking frog is pretty awesome!"

MARRIAGE

An actuary and her husband were happy for 20 years.
Sadly, they then met.

I just got married, and I'm scared of the statistics. I'm not sure
if I should be more worried about that 50% of marriages end
in divorce or that 50% of all marriages last.

My non-actuarial wife and I share a fantastic sense of humour.
We have to because, as an actuary, I don't have one.[36]

What does an actuary's wife do when she can't get to sleep?
She asks her husband, "Tell me again what you do at work."

In a worker's compensation insurance, the pension is given to
the surviving spouse until death or remarriage.
Hence getting married again is actuarially equivalent to
death.[37]

---

[36] John Lee

[37] Attributed to Ralph Garfield.

My new wife told me I'm terrible in bed.
I told her it's statistically inappropriate to draw a conclusion
from less than a minute's worth of data.

What does an actuary use for birth control?
Their personality.

My wife thinks I'm cheating on her.
It's affair assumption.

DIVORCE

Extensive modelling by a team of actuaries has shown the most significant factor leading to divorce is marriage. Since everyone who has divorced has first been married.

An actuary asked his wife, "Why do you always carry my photo with you whenever you go to work?"
His wife replied, "Because whatever difficulties I face during the day, I just look at your photo and realise that things don't seem so bad...."
The actuary sighed with delight.
Then his wife continued, "... as I think to myself, 'no problem I encounter can be bigger than this one.'"

Did you hear about the actuary who
blamed arithmetic for her divorce?
Her husband put two and two together.

FAMILY

An actuary gave birth to identical twins,
and she called them *dy* and *dx*.
However, people couldn't differentiate between them.

My daughter used to be terrible at graphing trig functions.
Fortunately, she's made excellent sines of improvement.

While watching their young son play, the wife remarks to her
husband, "He is such a sensitive child. Let's wait until he's
much older before telling him you're an actuary."

A son asked his father, "Dad, how did you decide on our
names?" The father replied, "Well, we named both of you after
our favourite things. For example, your sister is called Rose, as
that's your mum's favourite flower. Why do you ask,
VLOOKUP?"[38]

---

[38] John Lee

My son is cold and calculating.
I've turned the heating off whilst he does his maths
homework.

Did you hear about the actuary who had two kids,
five and eight?
He's not very good at naming things.

My son asked me if he should take algebra, and I said it was a
difficult question to answer.
There are just too many variables involved.

How do actuaries reprimand their kids?
"If I've told you n times, I've told you $n+1$ times."

How do children answer the question: "How old are you?"
Normal children: I'm 6 years old.
Children of actuaries: I'm 6 years last birthday old.[39]

---

[39] John Lee

JOKES ACTUARIES TELL THEIR CHILDREN

The problem with math puns is that arithmetic jokes are pretty basic, algebra jokes are usually formulaic, calculus jokes are mostly derivative, and trigonometry jokes are too graphic.

But I suppose the odd statistics joke is an outlier.

NUMBER

Why do people find the absolute value of zero so amusing?

|0|

I asked my German friend if she knew the square root of 81.

She said nein.

Last night I was thinking about 0.999999 as I was sleeping.
Turns out it was a recurring dream.[40]

Why did the actuary lose the fight against 1, 3, 5 and 7?
Because the odds were against him.

My teacher asked me if I had my own maths equipment.
I said "I have a broken abacus." She said "That doesn't count".

Never ask a felon to organise something numerically.
Not unless you're prepared to handle the con sequences.

---

[40] John Lee

ALGEBRA

Why were Adam and Eve thrown out of the polynomial
Garden of Eden?
They calculated the forbidden root.[41]

Why wasn't the hyperbola feeling sick?
Because it was asymptote-matic.

How do we know that the fractions x/c, y/c and z/c live
abroad?
Because they're all over c's.

What did the policeman say when it arrested the function?
"You have the right to domain silent."[42]

With great power...
comes greater difficulty in factorising the polynomial.

---

[41] John Lee

[42] John Lee

CALCULUS

What is the derivative of Amazon?

Amazon Prime.

What do you call an integral that hates derivatives?

An anti-derivative.

Why was the calculus conference so long?

The speakers kept going off on tangents.

Which is more important to learn:

derivatives or anti-derivatives?

Anti-derivatives. They're integral to your success.

What's $\int \frac{1}{cabin} \, dcabin$?

Natural log cabin.[43]

---

[43] For the picky actuaries who say that I've forgotten the C, the answer is natural log houseboat.

GEOMETRY

My pet snake is 3.14 metres long.

It's a pi-thon.

What do you call a nine-sided polygon

that wants to stay anonymous?

Anonagon.

Why was the maths teacher late for school?

She took the rhombus.

Why did the teacher give the rectangle a detention?

Because it said a square word.

TRIGONOMETRY

I've been reading a textbook about the shape of the sine and cosine functions.

It has its ups and downs.

Why is zero equal to one?

Cos 0 equals 1.

Why don't mathematicians graduate from university with degrees?

Because they prefer radians.

How does a deaf actuary communicate?

By using sine language.

STATS & PROBABILITY

What insect is good at statistics?

Probabili-bees.

What's smarter than the average bear?

50% of all bears.

Why is it difficult to study statistics in Afghanistan?

Because of the tally-ban.

One statistician asked another how she felt after a fiery snowmobile accident. The second replied, "Well, my hair was on fire, and my toes got frostbite, but on average, I felt fine."

I asked a German friend to draw me

a circular probability diagram.

He said, "Venn?"

I said as soon as you can.

ACTUARIES
&
ACCOUNTANTS

In God we trust.
All others must supply data.

W. Edwards Deming

ACCOUNTANTS ON ACTUARIES

An actuary is someone who aspired to become an accountant,
but just didn't have the personality for it.

What do you call an actuary who marries an accountant?
A social climber.

What motivates some accountants to become actuaries?
When bookkeeping excites them just too much.

How do actuaries liven up their office party?
They ask an accountant to attend.

ACTUARIES ON ACCOUNTANTS

CPA

~~Certified Public Accountant~~

Can't Pass Actuarial

CA

~~Chartered Accountant~~

Can't Add

ACA

~~Associate Chartered Accountant~~

Also Can't Add

What's the difference between an actuary and an accountant?

About £45,000.[44]

---

[44] John Lee, but probably not original.

Why did the accountant become so excited after completing a jigsaw puzzle in only 49 weeks?
Because on the box it said 9-12 Years.

Why is it that accountants laugh three times when they hear a joke?
They laugh once when it's told to them, once when it's explained to them, and once when they finally understand it.

My accountant friend has now borrowed seven of my books and not returned any of them.
I think she's a professional bookkeeper.

Why don't accountants spend any time in the mornings staring out of the office windows?
Because then they'd have nothing to do at lunchtime.

An actuary entered a bar with his crocodile on a leash.
"Do you serve accountants?" he asked.
The bartender replied, "Of course."
"Great," said the actuary. "I'll have a beer, and my pet crocodile will have an accountant."

Why did God invent accountants?

So actuaries could at least have someone to laugh at.

Why did the accountant spend three hours staring at her glass
of orange juice?

Because the carton said "Concentrate".

Why don't they give accountants coffee breaks
longer than 10 minutes?

It takes far too long to retrain them.

Why do actuaries take an instant dislike to accountants?

To save time later.

What can you say about an accountant who is drooling out of
both sides of their mouth?

They are level-headed.

Why couldn't the accountant add 10 and seven on a
calculator?

They couldn't find the 10 key.

An actuary, an old woman, an accountant and a beautiful blonde are travelling on a train. The train enters a tunnel, the lights go out and in the dark there is a loud slap. The compartment lights up and they see a red five-finger mark on the accountant's face.

The old woman thinks: perhaps the accountant touched the blonde, so she quite rightly gave him a slap.

The blonde thinks: perhaps the accountant tried to touch me but touched the old woman by mistake, so she rightly slapped him.

The accountant thinks: perhaps the actuary touched the blonde in the dark and she slapped me by mistake.

The actuary thinks: I can't wait for the train to enter the next tunnel so I can give that accountant another slap.

One day, Jane, the accountant and two colleagues were heading to a client meeting. Just after they'd parked and locked the car, Jane realised that they'd left the keys inside.

"How on earth are we going to fix this?" asked Jane.

"We could try using a coat hanger to unlock the door," the first accountant replied.

"How about trying to pry the door open," suggested the second accountant

Jane replied, "Well, whatever we do, we'd best hurry because a storm's fast approaching, and the top is still down."

How many accountants are needed to calculate the present value of an annuity?

Three.

One to calculate each payment's amount, one to determine the right account to record the payments in, and the last one to find an actuary and ask them how to calculate it.

"We are all here today to show the world that accountants aren't stupid," declares the host of the accountant's convention. "Could I please have a volunteer?" An accountant joins him on the platform. The host asks him, "What's 18 add 18?" After about 20 seconds, the accountant replies, "Thirty."

Clearly, everyone is understandably disappointed. But then the audience of 60,000 accountants yell out, "Give him another chance, give him another chance!" The host responds, "Well, seeing as we've gone to the effort of getting all 60,000 of you here for the worldwide press, I suppose we can give him one more go."

The host asks the volunteer a simpler question, "What's 7 add 7?" After nearly 40 seconds, the accountant answers, "Twenty?" The host sighs, and the accountant starts crying, but the audience yells, "Give him another chance, give him another chance."

Unsure whether he is making things worse, the host eventually agrees, "OK! Just one more try. What's 2 add 2?" A full minute of silence passes, before the accountant eventually opens his eyes and declares, "Four."

Pandemonium erupts across the stadium as all 60,000 accountants leap to their feet and yell, "Give him another chance, give him another chance!"

An actuary would entertain herself by running over accountants. Whenever she saw an accountant walking by the road, she would swerve, mount the pavement to strike them then veer back onto the road after enjoying the satisfying "THUMP".

In case you're wondering, she recognised them by their pale complexion and grey clothes.

A priest was hitchhiking one day, and the actuary thought she would do a good turn. She pulled the car over and said, "I'll give you a lift, Father." The priest got into the car and the actuary continued down the road.

A little later, the actuary spotted an accountant walking and naturally swerved to mount the kerb. But then she remembered there was a priest in the car with her, so she swerved away, narrowly missing the accountant. However, she still heard a loud "THUD".

Not understanding where that noise came from, she glanced in her mirrors and when she saw nothing, she turned to the priest and said, "I'm sorry, Father, I almost hit that accountant."

"It's okay," replied the priest. "I got him with the door."

In a bar, a man leans over to the man next to him and asks, "Do you want to hear an accountant joke?"

The man beside him scowls, "Before you share that joke, you'd better know that I'm an accountant and I'm 6 foot 2 and weigh 220 pounds. And the man sitting on my right is also an accountant, and he's 6 foot 4 and weighs 240 pounds. So, are you still planning on telling me that joke now?"

The first man answers, "Nah, I don't want to explain it twice."

ACTUARIES
& OTHER
PROFESSIONS

An economist is an expert who will
know tomorrow why the things
he predicted yesterday didn't
happen today.

Laurence J. Peter

CFA

~~Chartered Financial Analyst~~
Certified Failed Actuary

A physicist, a chemist, and an actuary walk into an office to discover the rubbish bin is on fire.

"Listen to me!" shouts the physicist. "We need to cool the materials until their temperature is lower than the ignition temperature, at which point the fire will be extinguished. Let's put it in the fridge."

"No!" says the chemist. "Listen to me! We can extinguish the fire by removing the oxygen supply as then it will lack one reactant. Let's cover the bin instead."

While the physicist and chemist argue about what to do, the actuary is running around the office, setting fire to the remaining office bins.

"What the hell are you doing??" they shout.

The actuary replies, "Getting an adequate sample size!"

A group of engineers are struggling to determine a flagpole's height with only a tape measure at their disposal, as the tape keeps falling down every time they try to place it up the pole.

An actuary walks by and asks the others what the problem is. They explain the situation and the actuary immediately removes the pole from its hole, places it on the ground, and measures it.

After the actuary has left, one engineer says to the others: "That's so typical of these actuaries! We needed the height, and she gave us the length!"

An engineer, a physicist, and an actuary were travelling across Scotland on a train. Whilst looking out the window, the engineer notices a single black sheep in a field and comments, "I see Scottish sheep are black."

The physicist retorts, "No. You mean that some sheep in Scotland are black."

The actuary rolls his eyes and says, "No. All we know is that in Scotland, there is at least one sheep and that at least one of its sides is black."

A doctor, a lawyer and an actuary have made it through to the final FBI entrance test and are all sitting nervously in a waiting room.

The lawyer is summoned first, given a gun and instructed to execute the spy in the next room. When the lawyer enters the room, he observes a person in a hood, handcuffed to a chair. The lawyer lifts the hood, discovers his wife underneath, and refuses to shoot her. Consequently, the lawyer fails the test and is dismissed.

The doctor is summoned next, given a gun and instructed to execute the spy in the next room. When the lawyer enters the room, she observes a person in a hood, handcuffed to a chair. The doctor lifts the hood, discovers her husband underneath, and refuses to shoot him. Consequently, the doctor also fails the test and is dismissed.

Finally, they summon the actuary, give him a gun and instruct him to execute the spy in the next room. The actuary enters the room, and a gunshot is heard, followed by the sounds of a struggle. Finally, the actuary exits and says, "Someone loaded the gun with blanks, so I was forced to choke her to death."

A Hindu, a Rabbi and an actuary were wandering through a remote countryside independently. Suddenly, a storm came up, and they each took refuge in a nearby house. The owner was happy for them to spend the night, but only had room for two in the house - so he offered the barn to the third.

The Hindu volunteered to sleep in the barn. About ten minutes later, there was a knock at the door. It was the Hindu - "I can't sleep there. There's a cow in the barn! In my religion, cows are sacred, and it just wouldn't be right."

The Rabbi volunteered to be the one who slept in the barn. Ten minutes later, there was a knock at the door. It was the Rabbi - "In my religion pigs are dirty, and there's a pig in the barn! I'm afraid I can't sleep there either."

The Actuary agreed, given the religious issues, to spend the night in the barn. About ten minutes later, there was a knock at the door.

It was the cow and the pig.

An actuary, a biologist, a statistician and a physicist are sitting in a café opposite an abandoned building. A car arrives, and two people get out and walk into the building. A couple of minutes later, they notice three people leaving the building.

"The measurement was inaccurate," states the physicist.

The biologist exclaims, "We've just seen reproduction in action!"

The statistician says, "This lies within the margin of error."

The actuary says, "If exactly one person now enters, the building will be empty again."

A physicist, an engineer, and an actuary go on a hunting trip. As they walk through the woods, they see a deer in a clearing.

The physicist considers the distance to the target, the speed of the bullet and how much it will drop by, but assumes a vacuum. So when she fires her rifle, her shot misses the deer by four feet to the left.

The engineer sighs. "You failed to account for the wind." He aims his rifle by adding a fudge factor for the speed and direction of the wind and fires. But his fudging meant he missed the deer by four feet to the right.

The actuary excitedly claps her hands as, on average, they'd hit it.

Five surgeons were discussing which type of patient is the best to operate on. "Actuaries are the greatest because everything inside them is numbered," the first surgeon explains.

The second surgeon replies, "Nah! Librarians are by far the best, since everything is arranged alphabetically inside."

"Electricians are where it's at," the third surgeon says, "It's all colour-coded inside!"

The fourth surgeon interjects, "I prefer lawyers. They've got no heart, no backbone, and are gutless. Furthermore, their ass and their head are interchangeable."

"Engineers are my favourite," added the fifth surgeon, who'd been quietly sitting in the corner listening to the others. "They always understand when you've got a couple of parts left over after the op."

On a long flight, an actuary and a lawyer find themselves seated next to each other. The lawyer leans over and asks the actuary, "Would you like to play a light-hearted game?" The actuary just wants to sleep, so she politely declines and turns towards the window and closes her eyes.

The lawyer persists, "It's lots of fun, all we do is take turns asking each other a question, and pay £5 to the questioner if we don't know the answer."

Again, she declines, turns back to the window and closes her eyes. Frustrated, the lawyer says, "How about you pay me £5 if you don't know the answer, and I'll pay you £500 if I don't know the answer?"

This catches the actuary's attention, and she agrees to play the game, figuring that the lawyer will just keep on nagging.

The lawyer goes first, "What goes up but never comes down?"

Without saying a word, the actuary opens her purse, takes out a £5 note, and gives it to the lawyer.

"Now it's your turn," says the lawyer. "What goes up a hill on three legs but comes down on four?" she asks the lawyer.

Perplexed, the lawyer pulls out his laptop and searches the internet. But he can't find the answer. Exasperated, he emails all his work colleagues and friends, but none of them can help.

After about an hour of frustration, he wakes the actuary and hands her £500. The actuary politely takes the money, turns back to the window and closes her eyes.

The lawyer is more than irritated by this, so he shakes the actuary and asks, "So, what's the answer?"

Without saying a word, the actuary opens her purse, gives the lawyer £5, and promptly goes back to sleep.

There was a business owner conducting interviews for a managerial position. A simple mathematics question was used to warm up the candidates: "What's two add two?"

The first interviewee was a mathematician who replied, "With this short proof I can quickly show it equals 4."

The second interviewee was an engineer, who answered, "4, but let's say 6, to be on the safe side."

A physicist answered, "4.0." whereas an astrophysicist replied, "It's in the magnitude of $1{\times}10^{1}$."

A statistician answered "4 with a standard error of 0.01."

A lawyer was the fifth applicant. She replied, "Two and two was declared to be four in the case of Johnson vs Smith."

The actuarial candidate grilled the interviewer, "What are your assumptions underlying your number system?"

The last applicant was an accountant who shut the door, leaned close to the desk and whispered, "What do you want it to be?"

Four passengers on a plane about to crash are the President, the Pope, a lawyer and an actuary. However, there are only three parachutes available.

"As President, I should have one," stated the President. The Pope replied, "Me, too, as I'm the Pope."

"Well, if you want help suing the airline properly, you'll need me to escape," added the lawyer. But the actuary objected, "Wait, who's going to calculate the insurance premiums?"

While they stopped to consider this, the plane crashed. [45]

Three statisticians and three biologists meet on a train on their way to a conference. The biologists gripe about the price of train tickets, so the statisticians share their cost-cutting technique. The statisticians cram themselves into a toilet when they hear the inspector coming. Tickets, please!" says the inspector as he knocks on the toilet door. The inspector stamps and returns the single ticket that the statisticians slid under the door. The biologists are awestruck.

On the train journey back from the conference, the biologists decide they are as bright as the statisticians, so they buy only one ticket, but the statisticians reply, "Well, we have no ticket at all." Unfortunately, the biologists hear the inspector's voice

---

[45] Attributed to Andy McGee.

before they can ask any questions. This time it's the biologists cramming themselves into a toilet. However, it's not the inspector knocking on the door saying "Tickets please!" but one of the statisticians who followed them! She takes the ticket the biologists slide under the door, and then she and her colleagues cram themselves into a different toilet and wait for the real ticket inspector.

The moral: "Never use a statistical technique that you don't fully understand."

An actuary, statistician and mathematician are standing in front of an "available" woman, who - for a bit of fun - positions herself exactly 2.00m away from them.

She says, "Take a 1.00m step, then a 0.50m step, then 0.25m step, and keep stepping, but always half the length of your previous step. If you can reach me, you can have me.

The mathematician bursts into tears because he knows that the distance he can cover is asymptotically 2.00m but never actually reaches 2.

The statistician knows about asymptotes but figures there is a non-zero probability that he might still reach 2m.

The actuary smiles, and the two reprimand him for not knowing about infinite conversing series, but he explains, "I might not reach 2.00m, but I will get close enough for all practical purposes."

Two underwriters boarded a plane. The first sat in the window seat while the other took the middle seat.

An actuary boarded the plane shortly before take-off and sat in the aisle seat adjacent to the two underwriters. The actuary took off his shoes, wiggled his toes and was just getting comfortable when the underwriter in the window seat said, "Excuse me, I need to get up and fetch a Coke."

"No worries," said the actuary. "I'll fetch it for you." While the actuary was away, one underwriter spat in his left shoe.

When the actuary returned with the Coke, the other underwriter remarked, "That looks great. I'm going to get one too." Once again, the actuary kindly went to get it, and this time the other underwriter spat in the actuary's right shoe while the actuary was away.

Once the actuary returned, everyone relaxed and enjoyed the flight. As the plane touched down, the actuary put his shoes on and realised what had happened.

The actuary sighed and asked, "How much longer will we continue this fight between our professions? This hostility? This spitting in shoes and urinating in drinks?"

JOKES ACTUARIES TELL ON HOLIDAYS

Fun is like life insurance; the older you get, the more it costs.

Kin Hubbard

HALLOWEEN

How do ghosts solve quadratic equations?

By completing the scare.

What estimator did the timid ghost use to haunt his house?

Least Scares.

How did the discrete distribution die?

It was Poisson-ed.

Who do you think my financial advisor will be for Halloween?

PENNY-WISE.

CHRISTMAS

What's an actuary's favourite part of Christmas?
Calculating their present value.[46]

Why aren't all bearded men in red suits Santa?
Because correlation doesn't imply Claus-ality.

What did actuarial Santa say?

H_0, H_0, H_0.[47]

---

[46] John Lee

[47] H_0 is the abbreviation for a null hypothesis.

EAT, STUDY, SLEEP

Insomnia sharpens your math skills because you spend all night calculating how much sleep you'll get if you're able to fall asleep right now.

I WORK ALL DAY. I STUDY ALL NIGHT.

What's black and white and has lots of problems?
An actuarial exam.[48]

Why can't marsupials become actuaries?
They don't meet the koalafications.

The actuarial exam I just sat had 101 questions. I thought,
"That's an odd number of questions."

I don't know why student actuaries get so upset about the
exams. I slept like a baby the night before my actuarial exams.
I woke every two hours crying.

One student actuary asks a qualified actuary,
"Would you sit my exam for me?"
The qualified actuary replies,
"Absolutely not, it just wouldn't be right."
The student replies, "Well, you could try anyway."

---

[48] John Lee but probably not original.

One day, an actuary is walking in the woods when he comes across an old lamp. A genie materialises when he picks it up and rubs it.

"I am a very powerful genie, capable of fulfilling your treasured wish. But just the one wish."

The actuary is extremely compassionate, produces a map from his pocket, and says, "Well, my heartfelt wish is that you resolve the Arab - Israeli conflict."

The genie says, "That's a tough one. They've been fighting for many generations, and nobody has been able to come up with a lasting, peaceful solution. I don't think I could solve that problem. You should wish for something else. "

The actuary is understanding and says, "OK. I would love to be able to complete my office work, study for my exams and still have a social life. Could you help me resolve this?"

After a long silence, the genie eventually responds, "Let me take another look at that map."

CALCULUS

A function and a differential operator meet in a dark, narrow alley.

"Get out of my way," says the differential operator,

"or I'll differentiate you until you're nothing."

"I'm not scared," retorted the function, "because I'm e^x."

"Yeah, well I'm d/dy."

Did you hear about the actuarial student who was struggling with stochastic calculus?

It was deriving them crazy.[49]

Where do actuaries go when they get sick?

The L'Hôpital.

My old car was like e^x.

You can derive it all you want,

but you're not going to get anywhere.

---

[49] John Lee but probably not original.

At a party, every function of x is present. Everyone is having a good time, mingling, chatting and dancing, with the exception of e^x who is sitting alone at the bar looking despondent. The other functions notice this and ask, "Hey e^x, why don't you integrate with us?"

"There's no point," e^x replies, "it wouldn't make any difference!"

STATISTICAL DISTRIBUTIONS

Why do we use phi (φ) to represent the standard normal
distribution?
Phi not?[50]

I attempted to conduct an experiment to determine the
impact dehydration has on the amount of urine produced by
humans.
However, the p-value was just too low.

$\bar{X}$ is where statisticians go when their work
drives them to drink.

What did the Gamma distribution say to the Chi-square
distribution when they were in trouble?
We're skewed.

Outgoing actuaries do not wait for moments,
they generate them.

---

[50] John Lee

I never thought population statistics would turn me on...

...but I've come to my census.

Why do statisticians become Bayesian after a few drinks?

Because they start making inferences from their posteriors.

What distribution do actuaries use to model

the height of ghosts?

The paranormal distribution.[51]

Two unbiased estimators were enjoying a few beers in a bar.

The first one asks, "How are you enjoying married life?" The

other replies, "It's OK, but you lose a degree of freedom!"

What kind of probability distribution smokes marijuana?

Joint distributions.[52]

---

[51] John Lee but probably not original.

[52] John Lee

What did the z distribution have to say about the t distribution?

You might look like me, but you're just not normal.

There's something fishy about the Poisson distribution.[53]

What test rejects a false hypothesis with the words:

"I pity the fool!"?

The Mr T Test.[54]

Statisticians who try to explain confidence intervals to me drive me crazy.

95% of the time I have no idea what they're talking about.

What's the difference between a statistician and a mathematician?

Statistically, no one cares.

---

[53] John Lee. Poisson is French for fish.

[54] John Lee. Mr T is an American actor with the catchphrase "I pity the fool!"

Regression is a powerful forecasting technique.
Economists using it have predicted 10 of the last 2 recessions.

When travelling to work, the mode of transport for a
statistician is usually the same as the means of transport.

Statistical parameters are all Greek to me.[55]

Which discrete distribution couldn't afford to buy lunch?
Bi-no-mial.

What do you call a statistical estimator with two butts?
Biased.[56]

In statistics, bigger sample sizes produce more reliable
averages.
I guess the n's justify the means.

---

[55] John Lee but probably not original.

[56] John Lee. Biased sounds like bi assed.

The Poisson distribution has a step-function for its CDF.
Sadly, it never knew its real function.[57]

I gathered a large amount of data trying to disprove
confirmation bias.
The results were just what I expected.

What do statisticians call a defective butter substitute?
A margarine of error.

What is the proper term for a tea party with more than
30 people?
A Z party.[58]

What is it called when a statistician
gives out clothes secretly?
Discreet uniform distribution.

---

[57] John Lee. Had a step-function like a step-dad as their real dad left.

[58] A t distribution with a sample size of at least 30 is considered be the same as the normal for all practical purposes.

Distributions may be dull, but they do have their moments.

What does a statistical DJ do to raise the crowd's spirit?

He drops the Bayes.[59]

Does the Poi(3.14) distribution have a pi-rate?[60]

The ultimate statistical put-down:

Your mother is so mean, she has no standard deviation!

What do you call an excited geometric distribution?

A hypergeometric.[61]

I discovered the secret of randomness.

It's not what you expect.

---

[59] John Lee. Bayes sounds like bass and "drop the bass" is a term used in electronic music to describe a sudden change in the bass line after a climatic build up.

[60] John Lee. The parameter of the Poisson distribution is the rate. 3.14 is the approximate value of pi, therefore Poi(3.14) has a pi rate.

[61] John Lee

What do you do if you calculate the analysis of variance incorrectly?

Have ANOVA go.[62]

In a bar, two random variables were chatting. They believed they were discrete, but I could hear them talking continuously.

An actuary (who was clearly lost) walks into a bar and as she turns to leave (before anyone notices), she sees two large pieces of meat stuck to the ceiling. The bartender (recognising the actuary by how out of place she was) says, "I bet you £500 you can't touch that meat without using a chair or anything else."

The actuary quickly estimates her chances before refusing, "No, I can't do it. The steaks are too high."

What is the one question the Cauchy distribution hates being asked?

Got a moment?[63]

---

[62] John Lee but probably not original. ANOVA stands for analysis of variance.

[63] The Cauchy distribution, unlike other distributions, has no moments.

Two homeless guys were sitting in a bar, moaning about how poor they were. "I'm so broke," said one of them.

At that moment, Bill Gates entered the bar.

"Good news," replied his friend. "On average, everyone in this bar just became millionaires."

Two actuaries were discussing which probability distribution they liked the most.

"There's something really special about the Gaussian distribution, don't you think?" said the first actuary.

"Oh no," the second actuary replied. "That's just normal."

How did the underage random variable get into the club?

By showing a fake i.i.d.

FINANCIAL MATHEMATICS

I used to enjoy calculating accumulated values,
but then I lost interest.

What sound does hitting someone over the head with
company capital make?
WACC![64]

What's the wettest annuity?
An annuity dew.[65]

Why did the lonely actuary buy some shares?
Because he wanted to have some company.

---

[64] John Lee. WACC is Weighted Average Cost of Capital – which is the average cost to a company of raising finance. It also sounds like whack.

[65] John Lee. An annuity due is a series of regular payments paid in advance, *ie* at the beginning of period.

Why do actuaries always purchase exactly the same socks?
To avoid mismatching risk.[66]

What do risk conscious pirates say?
VaRRRRRRRRRRRRR![67]

[66] John Lee

[67] John Lee

MORTALITY

Why was the actuary calculating mortality probabilities on the floor?
She was trying not to use tables.[68]

I'd planned to write my will today, but then I thought, life's too short.

What do actuaries look for when buying clothes?
Goodness-of-fit.[69]

What tables do actuaries refer to when something unexpected happens?
Contingency tables.[70]

---

[68] John Lee

[69] John Lee

[70] John Lee

What function is used to model an actuary's journey to work
each day?

A commutation function.

Actuary to accountant: "If q_7 is the probability of a 7-year-old
dying in the next year, what is q_8?"

Accountant: "A small country bordering Iraq?"[71]

Did you hear about the Native American actuary who named
his wigwam x?

It was his $\,_t p_x$.[72]

A student actuary was riding on the bus and reading
an article about mortality statistics.

Fascinated, she shares a fact with the passenger next to her,
"Did you know that with every breath I take, someone dies?"

The passenger turns to her and says,

"Have you tried mouthwash?"

---

[71] q_8 sounds like Kuwait.

[72] John Lee. A wigwam is another name for a tepee. So $\,_t p_x$ sounds like tepee x.

What do you call an actuary being shy about
what happened yesterday?
Retrospective reserve.[73]

---

[73] John Lee

PAYBACK – I MEAN PAYING IT BACK TO THE PROFESSION

What did the actuary think of volunteering for the Profession?

She said, "I wouldn't do it if they paid me."

Did you hear about the examiner with a nervous tic?[74]

Everyone got really good marks.

I always give 100%,

which is probably why I lost my job as an exam marker.

---

[74] In the UK, a tick is what Americans call a checkmark.

MEMES

Politicians use statistics in the same way that a drunk uses lamp-posts— for support rather than illumination.

Andrew Lang

ACTUARIAL TUTOR MEMES

DENIAL - of course I'll keep my social life!

ANGER - I just don't have time to fit it all in!

BARGAINING - I'll have a social life once I qualify!

DEPRESSION - I'll have no friends left once I qualify

ACCEPTANCE - I've got Excel, who needs friends?

THE 5 STAGES OF BECOMING AN ACTUARY

THINKING ABOUT BECOMING AN ACTUARY

STUDYING TO BECOME AN ACTUARY

John Lee
actuarialtutor.substack.com

MATH GRADUATES

ACTUARIAL PROFESSION

ACTUARIAL EXAMS

John Lee
ActuarialTutor.substack.com

ACTUARIES:
THE PERFECT DRESS DOES NOT EXI...

John Lee
ActuarialTutor.substack.com

ACTUARIES BE LIKE...

WHAT GIVES **ACTUARIes**
FEELINGS OF POWER

MONEY

STATUS

using pivot
tables

THAT mini HeART ATTACK
WHen You CAn'T FeeL one
oF THese in YouR PockeT

HOW TO CATCH AN ACTUARY

OTHER MEMES

Meme by tragiccomix. Used with their kind permission.

Just like any other profession...
Actuaries experience a roller coaster of emotions.

A boring day in the life of an Actuary

An exciting day in the life of an Actuary

Despite by best efforts, I cannot find the original author of this cartoon. Please get in contact if you can help out.

A DAY IN THE LIFE OF AN ACTUARY

Don't become a novelist;
be a statistician,
much more scope for the
imagination.

Mel Calman

INTERVIEW

Interviewer: What do you consider to be your st—

Guy: strengths? Making inferences from minimal data.

Interviewer: Okay, and your we—

Guy: Wheat Allergies? None whatsoever.

What's the biggest lie actuaries tell prospective candidates?

We have a great work life balance.[75]

During a recent job interview, the interviewer asked if I could perform under pressure.

I said, "No, but I can do Bohemian Rhapsody."

Interview question: What first attracted you to the salary of an actuary? [76]

---

[75] John Lee

[76] John Lee

Did you hear about the professional hockey player who quit
her job to become an actuary?

She wanted an off-ice job.

During my last job interview, I said I would give 110%.

Unfortunately, I was applying to be a statistician.

A young actuarial graduate, fresh out of University and
thinking he knows everything, applied for his first job.

At interview, the prospective employer asked him what
starting salary he was looking for.

The graduate replied, "Oh, I was thinking around £80,000 per
year, subject to other benefits."

The potential employer replied, "Well, how does this sound?

Six week's annual leave, 20% superannuation, paid expenses
to overseas conferences every year, home telephone calls
reimbursed, and a company car replaced every 20,000 miles,
starting with a Mercedes convertible."

The graduate sat up straight and tried not to look excited as
he said, "Wow. Are you joking?"

The employer replied,

"Yes. But you're the one who started it."

In the interview, they asked what drove me to
become an actuary.
I replied, "Uber."

After losing her Chief Actuary, the CEO of an insurance
company hires a recruitment firm to find a replacement.

After a while, they let her know that they have four candidates
ready for interview. The CEO shocks them by asking if any of
the candidates are missing an arm.

After reviewing their files, they confirm that they do have one
applicant with only one arm. The CEO instantly responds, "I'll
take them".

The head-hunters are baffled, so the CEO explains, "I'm
looking for an actuary who can make decisions. I'm tired of
hearing actuaries say, 'but on the other hand...'"

I saw an advertisement: actuarial trainee wanted £ 25,000 -
£30,000. I called them and said there's no need for them to
look any further. The answer is -£5000.

IN THE OFFICE

What's an actuary's definition of progress?
Starting the day with lots of problems,
but finishing with lots of problems in a spreadsheet.

I've started referring to my procrastination as
"non-value added time."
It helps me feel a bit better about myself.

How did the actuary take her revenge on the bad data?
She made an ex-sample of them.[77]

Someone left some plasticine on my desk.
I just don't know what to make of it.

How does an actuarial firm report the death of one of its
annuitants?
"Pensioner Releases Their Reserves".

---

[77] John Lee

I was sad to finish my data modelling project,
but all good things come to a trend.[78]

Data science is 80% preparing data,
and 20% complaining about preparing data.

All I do at work is prepare data by subtracting the average
number from the inputs.
It's demeaning.

---

[78] John Lee

OFFICE POLITICS

The actuarial department sent their boss
a "get better soon" card.
He's not sick; they just think he could do better.

Two actuaries are taken to a restaurant by their underwriter.
"What can I get for you, ma'am?" the waiter asked the
underwriter.
"I'll have the steak," she answered.
"And what about your vegetables?"
The underwriter responds, "They'll also have the steak."

Two senior actuaries are talking about sex.
The first says that sex is 75% work and 25% pleasure.
The second says that sex is 25% work and 75% pleasure.
At an impasse, they decide to ask their student actuary for his
opinion. "Sex is all pleasure," says the student.
"What makes you say that?" the senior actuaries ask.
The student replies, "Simple. If there is any work involved,
you two make me do it. "

What lets you know that a pricing actuary is getting soft?
When they actually listen to marketing before saying no.

A tourist discovers a butcher's shop on a cannibal-infested
island. The shop specialises in human brains and priced them
according to where they come from:

Actuary' Brains... £20/kg

Underwriters' Brains... £30/kg

Claims Adjusters' Brains... £60/kg

Insurance Executives' Brains... £150/kg

Insurance Salesmen's' Brains... £300/kg

The tourist read the sign and exclaimed, "Wow, those
insurance salesmen's brains must be something pretty special!"
"Are you joking?" retorted the butcher. "Do you know just
how many salesmen it takes to obtain a kilo of brains?"

Why is it that as business execs and salesmen earn more actuaries and data scientists?

Well, making the following two assumptions:

1. Time is Money.

2. Knowledge is Power.

We can explain this phenomenon using mathematical reasoning as follows:

Power = Work / Time

Substituting for Power and Time gives:

Knowledge = Work / Money.

Rearranging gives:

Money = Work / Knowledge.

Therefore, regardless of the quantity of work completed, this equation tells us that the less someone knows, the more money they'll earn.[79]

---

[79] Scott Adams, this is known as the "Dilbert Principle".

STATISTICAL ANALYSIS

According to a large survey of people who had played Russian roulette, it seems like the probability of dying is actually 0%.

Are you lazy?
Well, Statistically 3,732,473,619 people
don't bother reading that number.

The statistics on how drunk people walk are just staggering.

What do you call a friend who always estimates everything?
An approxi-mate.

Statistics show vegetarians live on average
ten years longer than meat eaters.
Ten long miserable years.

The Bureau of Incomplete Statistics reports that
one out of three.

Statistics show that 84% of actuaries are pedantic.

Well, 84.1%.

Statistics show that 6 out of 7 dwarves aren't happy

whereas 1 in 4 hobbits are merry.[80]

According to statistics, 80% of all fatal plane crashes happen
in the first 3 or last 8 minutes of the flight. However,
according to even more precise statistics, 100% of all fatal
plane crashes occur within the final 0.1 seconds of flight.

A pole was taken last month. Statistics show a large increase
in the kidnapping of Eastern Europeans.

An actuary analysed thousands of obituaries and on any given
day, according to their fitted model, deaths occur in
alphabetical order.

---

[80] In case you're confused, in Snow White and the 7 dwarves, only one of the
dwarves was named Happy. And in the Lord of the Rings, only one of the 4
hobbits was named Merry.

A recent study found that inadequate research renders between 0% and 100% of statistics meaningless.

Studies show that if you laid all the actuaries end to end around the earth, two-thirds would be under water.

According to a recent statistical study, the average human has a single breast and a single testicle.

According to statistics, someone is stabbed in London every 52 seconds. Poor guy.[81]

According to statistical analysis, one in every three people in a relationship cheats...

I just need to work out whether it's my wife or girlfriend.[82]

What are stadium statistics?
They are ballpark estimates.

---

[81] OK, it's actually every 3 hours to be realistic. However, it makes the joke that it's the same person getting stabbed every time a little less obvious...

[82] An actuary can probably never relate...

Statistics show teen pregnancy reduces dramatically after nineteen.

Statistically speaking, if you take the entire population of the world and cut them in half...

They'll die.

Accordion to a recent study, when replacing words with instruments, they tend to go unnoticed.[83]

---

[83] Take another look at the first word of the joke.

MODELS & PREDICTION

What do you call a sad generalised linear model?
A GLuM.[84]

What do you call a machine used to predict the answer to a
mathematical question before it has been proposed?
A calcuearlier.

If at first you don't succeed, try calling it version 1.0.

As an actuary I never make definitive predictions.
I never have and I never will.

In order to understand recursion...
One must first understand recursion.[85]

---

[84] John Lee

[85] Actuary Problem Dog

What do you call an actuary obsessed
with machine learning algorithms?
An Algo-holic.[86]

"You're going to talk about my fixation with predicting the
future again, aren't you?"
I stated to my therapist.
"Yes," she replied.
"I knew it!" I exclaimed.

What's square and disorganised?
A confusion matrix.[87]

Why did the actuary call her model rude names?
Sensitivity testing.[88]

---

[86] John Lee but probably not original.

[87] John Lee

[88] John Lee

The Actuary's Prayer (v3.01)

Our model, which art in nowhere.

Guessing be thy name.

Thy assumptions come,

Thy will be done in future as it was in the past.

Give us this day our premium rates,

and forgive us our lousy estimates,

as we forgive those who supply us with crappy data.

Lead us not into insolvencies,

and deliver us from auditors.

For thine is the #NAME?, #DIV/0! and #VALUE!,

forever and ever. Amen.[89]

---

[89] I'd genuinely love to know the author of this.

Interviewer: What kind of assumptions does your model use?

Actuary: Which model, Model 1 or Model 2?

Interviewer: Model 1

Actuary: Best estimate.

Interviewer: And Model 2?

Actuary: Best estimate.

Interviewer: And how many parameters do you use?

Actuary: In which model, Model 1 or Model 2?

Interviewer: Model 1

Actuary: 15 parameters, as that minimises the AIC.

Interviewer: And Model 2?

Actuary: 15 parameters, as that minimises the AIC.

Interviewer: And what did your model predict?

Actuary: Model 1 or Model 2?

Interviewer: Model 1

Actuary: 4%±1% return on our investments.

Interviewer: And Model 2?

Actuary: 4%±1% return on our investments.

Interviewer: (Annoyed) but why do you keep on asking if it's Model 1 or Model 2 when answers are just the same??

Actuary: Because Model 1 was written by me.

Interviewer: And Model 2?

Actuary: That was also written by me.[90]

---

[90] Idea by Greg Solomon, adapted by John Lee.

REPORTING/PRESENTING

My friend always helps me out with maps and diagrams by
pointing out what all the little symbols mean.

The guy is a legend.

Top actuarial presentation tip:

A bar chart should never be displayed during an AA
meeting[91].

I drew a graph for my report, expecting a straight line. But I
actually got a curve.

What a plot twist.

I'm trying to plot a good scattergraph from my data, but some
unknown person keeps adding more samples to it.

The plot thickens.

---

[91] As an actuary, you might need to be told that AA stands for Alcoholics
Anonymous and not Appointed Actuary...

WORK-LIFE BALANCE

Why do actuaries love Fridays?

They get the whole weekend to catch up on work.[92]

What do you call an actuary who always works through lunch,

takes only two days' holiday a year, is in the office every

weekend, and leaves every night after 10 pm?

Lazy.

What is an actuary's favourite thing about holidays?

There is less traffic on the way to work.

Why are actuaries so excited about Saturdays?

They get to wear casual attire to work.

What do you call an actuary that's caught up

on all their work?

Make believe.[93]

---

92 John Lee

93 John Lee

Why don't actuaries read novels?

As the only numbers found in the novels are the page numbers.[94]

How can you tell when an actuary is on holiday?

They're not wearing a tie at work and they come in after 8.30.

---

[94] If you thought "and chapter numbers" then you are also a pedantic actuary.

CALCULATORS

How can you tell when an actuary's having a mid-life crisis?
They get a faster calculator.

One of my colleagues at work swallowed her calculator. I stood
up for her when everyone else said she was a weirdo.
I told them, "She might be a bit weird,
but it's what's inside her that counts!"

I recently watched the James Bond movie about my
Japanese calculator.
"*Casio* Royale" [95]

What do American calculators and country music have in
common?
Both are produced by *Texas* instruments.

---

[95] John Lee

I keep cutting my fingers on my calculator.
That's the problem with using a *Sharp* calculator.[96]

Did you hear about the actuary who owned a
golden calculator?
He only uses it on special equations...

What do you call an actuary without a calculator?
Lonely.

Our supplier sent us a shipment of broken calculators.
Seriously, we just can't count on them at all anymore.

I don't know why we need a pocket calculator for the
actuarial exams. I only have a few pockets
and can easily count them myself.

My calculator is missing the minus button.
I guess it won't make any difference.

---

[96] John Lee

EXCEL

Next year I'm planning on giving up spreadsheets
for 40 days and 40 nights before Easter.
It's going to be Excel Lent.

What do Excel and hotel maids have in common?
They both spread sheets.

What do you call an actuary without a spreadsheet?
Lost.

What do Excel users style their hair with?
SUMPRODUCT().

What does a baby Excel sheet drink?
Formula.

How to you determine if an Excel sheet has an error?
You carry out a COLUMNoscopy.

Why does a spreadsheet look so lifelike?
Because it's made of cells.[97]

Why was the spreadsheet afraid of its chart?
Because it has multiple axes.

What do you call an ant that is very good at working
with spreadsheets?
Excel-ant.

Where do you go to get a drink in Excel?
The formula bar.

I can't produce quality work in Excel without receiving praise.
I really need the validation.

Recently, Excel and I have not been getting along.
We just don't have the same values.

---

[97] John Lee

What's an actuary's favourite Roman numeral?

XL.[98]

Why doesn't Excel respond to texts?

It prefers it when you COLUMN on their cell.

What do Excel and men have in common?

They both mistakenly believe something to be a date.

What do conspiracy theorists and actuaries have in common?

They both spread sheet.

How many Excel users are needed to correctly set a cell's number formatting?

Sunday January 01, 1900.

An actuary opens up their spreadsheet, only to find all the numbers missing. Her cat is sitting by the desk, looking smug. I don't know why she's so surprised; cats are good at knocking things off tables.

---

[98] John Lee

What do actuaries call their old mobile?
An ex-cell phone.[99]

What do you call using VBA coding to make money?
MACROeconomics.

I spent last night in a cell.
I dreamt I was in a spreadsheet.[100]

What's the difference between your ex and COUNT?
COUNT ignores your errors.

Who discovered the first Excel sheet?
Christopher COLUMNbus.

How do you find out where the actuarial murderer
buried the bodies?
Ask his ex-cell mate.[101]

---

[99] John Lee

[100] John Lee

[101] John Lee

I asked my mum whether she knew any excel formulae.

She said yeah, SUM.

What is Excel's favourite game?

Hide and Goal Seek.

Why was the spreadsheet crying?

Because it contained sensitive data.[102]

Did you hear about the actuary who went mad while trying to create a graph in Excel?

She completely lost the plot.[103]

What do you call an elephant that's been killed by a spreadsheet?

An excelephant.[104]

---

[102] John Lee

[103] John Lee

[104] John Lee

If you still have any concerns about using a talking
spreadsheet, you should just give it a try.
The results will speak for themselves.

What do you call a project spreadsheet with an error in?
A late night.[105]

Optimist: the glass is half full.
Pessimist: the glass is half empty.
Excel: the glass is 1st February.[106]

---

[105] John Lee

[106] Or January 2nd if you're using the American month/day/year system.

PENSIONS

There are worse things in life
than death
- have you ever spent an evening
with a pensions actuary?

Woody Allen (adapted)

What does an actuary call their retirement?
The aftermath.

Today's interview for the position of Kamikaze pilot went well.
Until I asked about the pension.

What's the difference between a pension savings account and a
musician?
One eventually matures and starts to make money.

What do you call the Terminator when he's retired?
The Exterminator.

I'm started a pension for my car's wheels.
It's a re-TYRE-ment fund.[107]

Why did the pension fund invest in tennis balls?
They have a high rate of return.

---

[107] John Lee

What kind of dodgy pension does a bridge need?

A sus-pension.[108]

What did the financial advisor say to the person with a small

pension pot?

Have you considered dying a bit earlier?

People say I wasted all of my pension savings buying pasta...

But I say it was worth every penne.

Why was the hippy disappointed upon retirement?

His pension pot wasn't what he expected.[109]

I just signed up for my company's 401k[110],

but I doubt I can run that far.

---

[108] John Lee

[109] John Lee

[110] A 401(k) is a retirement savings and investing plan that US employers offer.

What occurs when the Grim Reaper
is too busy to collect souls?
Death in deferment.

On a plane, travelling back from a conference, two actuaries
were discussing changes in pension regulations over a non-
actuary seated between them.
After more than an hour of this discussion, the passenger
between them offered to switch places so they could talk and
he could get to sleep.
One actuary commented to the other: "That's the first time a
pension regulation discussion ever kept anyone awake."

What does the pessimistic pension actuary think?
It's accrual world.[111]

---

[111] John Lee, but probably not original.

The chief financial officer calls the actuarial firm she has used for years and requests to speak with an actuary.

The receptionist transfers the CFO to the actuarial department, where the actuarial manager tells him,

"For the last time, you've changed to a money purchase scheme, so you don't need a Scheme Actuary."

"I know," the financial director replies.

"I just wanted to hear you say it again."

A man died, and the devil took him to his place of eternal torment. As he passed sulphurous pits and shrieking sinners, he saw a man he recognised as a boring pensions actuary snuggling up to a beautiful woman.

"That's not fair," he complained. "I face torment for all eternity, and that pensions actuary gets to spend his afterlife with a beautiful woman."

"Shut up!" the devil yelled as he jabbed the man with his pitchfork. "Who are you to argue about that woman's punishment?"

According to my calculations, with my current pension pot, I could live comfortably for the rest of my life.

As long as I die by next Friday.

LIFE ASSURANCE

Life insurers always tell you to keep in shape.
My grandmother, she started walking five miles a day when she was 60.
She's 97 today and we don't know where the hell she is.

Ellen DeGeneres

Why aren't endowment assurance plans very talkative?

Because they are highly reserved.

My wife and I purchased life insurance for each other.

So now it's just a waiting game.

Because I believe in reincarnation, my insurance provider
declined to reimburse my medical costs.

They claimed I had a pre-existing condition.

You know, my health insurance lets me be ill at ease.

My health insurance company is offering me a cheaper deal if I
promise not to eat shellfish.

It's called their No Clams Bonus.

Purchasing life insurance is actually a form of gambling

Me: I'll wager £100 that I'll die this year.

Company: £50,000 says you don't.

How do you know that you're becoming old?
Your insurance provider sends you only half a calendar.

The ideal name for a life insurance salesman would be...
Justin Case.

Do schizophrenics suffer from multiple decrements?

We have a great insurance policy at work. Have you read it?
The benefit is that if we die, our families no longer have to
pay the premiums.

The life insurance salesman questioned his client, "Are you
aware of what the current market value of your husband's life
insurance policy is?"
The woman replied, "What do you mean?"
"I mean, what you would get if your husband were to die?"
After giving it some thought, the woman grinned and replied,
"Probably a poodle."

Why was the life actuary in rehab?

Solvency abuse.[112]

Why didn't the actuary take out life insurance?

So someone would be upset when she died.[113]

How did the turtle reply to the insurance agent?

"No, I'm not interested in purchasing life insurance.

I'm already covered."

The other day, I noticed an underwater door with the sign:

"Actuarial Cetaceans Only".

Apparently, it was strictly for insurance porpoises.

A life insurance agent was filling out an application when she

reached the section about health history.

She asked the client how his grandpa had died.

"Peacefully in his sleep," the client said,

"Not shouting and screaming like his car's passengers."

---

[112] John Lee, but probably not original.

[113] John Lee

Life insurance is a weird concept.

This is how it works: you pay me money.

And when you die, I'll pay you money.

"You must be insane!" my boss exclaimed, "How can you issue

a 108 year old man a life insurance policy?"

"I did what you said," I replied, "I applied rigorous analysis,

and according to our data, and in the past five years,

not a single 108-year-old has died."

Why doesn't Santa provide his workers with health insurance?

Because they're all elf employed.

What's the biggest plus about retirement?

No more cold calls selling life insurance.

It doesn't make sense that you're statistically more likely to die

when you're older.

As the older you are, the more experience you have of not

dying.

A life insurance policy keeps you poor your entire life
so that you can die rich.

Four life insurance companies are in constant competition and
attempt to outdo one another with new advertising slogans.
The first company creates the tagline
"Coverage from the cradle to the grave."
The second company improves this with
"Womb to the tomb coverage."
The third company expands it to
"From sperm to the worm."
The fourth and final company had nearly given up trying to
better this when they hit upon
"Coverage from erection to resurrection."

Three actuaries were bragging about the service of their respective insurance companies.

"On Monday, when one of our policyholders died abruptly, we got the news that evening, processed the claim and had the money wired to his wife on Wednesday evening." boasted the first actuary.

The second actuary retorted, "Well when one of our policyholders died without warning on Monday, we learned of it in 2 hours and wired the money to them the same evening."

The third actuary remarked, "That's nothing. Our company is on the 12th floor of a tall office block.

One of our policyholders tripped and fell while cleaning a window on the 80th floor. We gave him his cheque as he passed our floor."

GENERAL / CASUALTY INSURANCE

Try this simple test: flip a coin, over and over again, calling out "Heads" or "Tails" after each flip. Half the time, people will ask you to please stop.

Jack Handey

Insurance is like a car, driven by the company president with the sales manager pressing the accelerator, the underwriter pumping the brake, the actuary peering out the back window giving directions and the claims department tossing money out of the sunroof.[114]

Did you hear about the new Karma insurance policy?
You get what you deserve.

Why was the stripper in need of additional insurance?
She had little to no coverage.

Earlier, I called my insurance agent and requested a quote.
He replied, "I have nothing to declare but my genius.
Oscar Wilde."
I retorted, "Sarcasm is the lowest form of wit. Oscar Wilde."

---

[114] Attributed to Fred Kilbourne and Rick Dorman

How is insurance like a hospital gown?
You're never covered as much as you believe.

Why should drivers who have never crashed their cars have
their insurance premiums increased?
They're driving wrecklessly.

What is the term for a friend who is employed at an insurance
company?
A friend with benefits.

Why was the baker unable to obtain insurance?
Due to her high whisk profile.

Lightning struck my local church, but the insurance company
refused to cover it.
According to the insurer, it was an act of God,
and hence, it was deliberate damage by the owner.

What's the best kind of motor insurance a snake can purchase?
Fully cobrahensive.

Why did the insurance company refuse to insure the high-wire artist?

Because she had an outstanding balance.

Why are politicians unable to obtain insurance?

Too much lie-ability.

A man wanted to insure his wooden leg against fire.
The first actuary quoted a premium of £500 *pa*, assuming the
leg burns once every 20 years and the leg's value was £10,000,
whereas a second actuary quoted only a premium of £50 *pa*.
"How did you calculate such a low premium?" the man asked.
"It's just given in the fire schedule rating table," she answered,
"a wooden structure equipped with a sprinkler at the top."

Why did the motor insurance pricing actuary set such a low premium on a "Fire and Theft" policy?
Because what kind of thief would steal a burnt car?

What do you call the time between an actuary being told a joke and them actually laughing?
IBNR.[115]

Yesterday, I called to renew my car insurance.
"Do you own any pets?" the lady on the phone asked just as I was about to hand up.
"Yes," I replied, "I have a dog."
"Would you like to insure him as well?" She asked.
I replied, "Not really. He can't drive."

I just saved loads of money on my motor insurance by switching
...my car into reverse and driving away from the accident.

---

[115] Mary Pat Campbell

At 2 am, I noticed people drinking coffee in the service
station.
Have they not seen the road safety campaigns?
People falling asleep at the wheel cause one-fifth of all
accidents. That means people staying awake caused
four-fifths of all accidents!
They're the real killers.

Why did the insurer refuse to pay the fisherman when his boat
capsized and all the fish swam away?
They said it was an act of cod.

I'm planning a camping trip but, to be honest, I'm not
impressed with my travel insurance.
Apparently if my tent is stolen during the night, it turns out
I'll no longer be covered.

What triangles can't actuaries catch?
Run-off triangles.[116]

---

[116] John Lee

An underwriter and an actuary are watching the news at ten.
There's a story about a man on a window ledge who says he's
going to jump.
"I'll bet you £50 he doesn't jump." wagers the underwriter.
"I'll take the bet," the actuary replies.
After a few minutes, they see that the man does indeed jump.
"Don't worry." says the actuary as the underwriter pulls out his
wallet, "I saw it on the news at six, so it's not really fair."
"So did I," the underwriter replies, "but I never expected it to
happen twice."

An insurance convention is taking place in a hotel when a
drunk enters the lounge, intending to cause havoc.
He yells, "I think all claims adjusters are thieves, and if you
don't like it, come on up here and do something about it!"
A man immediately runs up to the drunk and shouts, "Hey!
You retract that statement right now!"
"Why?" the drunk responds with a sneer,
"Are you a claims adjuster?"
"No," the man replies, "I'm a thief."

Insurance is a form of gambling where we bet on our chance
of avoiding disaster and only win when we lose.

Sue called the insurance company when her barn burned down.

"I'd like the £80,000 I had that barn insured for."

"Unfortunately, that's not how it works," the agent replied, "First, we'll assess the value of the old barn and based on that, we'll then supply a new barn of equivalent value."

Sue paused for a moment while she considered this,

"Well, if that's how it works, I'd like to cancel my insurance policy on my husband!"

A TRUE STORY
THAT READS LIKE A JOKE:

In Charlotte, North Carolina, a man insured his case of very rare and expensive cigars against.... wait for it... fire.

The man filed a claim within a month, after consuming his entire stockpile of exquisite cigars and without having paid any premiums.

In his claim, he stated the cigars had been lost in "a series of small fires."

Since the man had obviously just smoked the cigars, the insurer refused to pay the claim.

He took the company to court and won his case.

The judge ruled the insured was entitled to compensation from the company for his loss because the policy guaranteed the cigars were insurable against fire without defining what was meant by "unacceptable fire."

The insurance company paid the man $15,000 for the rare cigars he lost in "the fires" instead of appealing the judge's decision, which would have been time-consuming and costly.

But the insurance company reported him for 24 counts of arson after he'd cashed his cheque.

Using his testimony from the previous case and his insurance claim, the man was found guilty of purposely setting the rare cigars on fire and fined $24,000 and sentenced to 2 years in jail.

CONSULTING
ACTUARIES

Mathematicians are like Frenchmen:
whatever you say to them, they
translate it into their own
language, and forthwith it means
something entirely different.

Johann Wolfgang von Goethe

A consulting actuary is someone who asks you for your watch, tells you the time and then charges a lot of money for the privilege!

How do you make a group of consultant actuaries smile for a photo?
Just say, "Fees".

Did you hear about the actuarial consulting firm run by cannibals?
They charge their clients an arm and a leg.

What's the difference between a consulting actuary and an angry rhinoceros?
The consulting actuary charges more!

A consulting actuary is someone who, when asked the time, tells you how to build a watch.

My consulting actuary friend is so mean,

she always laughs at my expense.[117]

A consulting actuary and his client sat down together for the

first time.

"I desperately need your help to interpret the significant

three-way interaction in our models. What are your fees?"

asked the client.

"Two hundred pounds for three questions," replied the

actuary.

"Isn't that a little steep?"

"Not at all. Now, what's your third question?"[118]

Why did the cannibal consulting actuary get reprimanded?

For buttering up his clients.

What do a pelican, a vulture, and a consulting actuary

have in common?

They all have long bills.

---

[117] John Lee, but probably not original.

[118] John Lee, but probably not original.

What do you call a consulting actuary
who doesn't have an opinion?
No-one knows.

An actuary dies and is met at the gates of heaven by St. Peter. "Welcome. Let me know your name and occupation and we'll get you booked in."

"I'm John Smith and I was an actuary."

"What sort of actuary were you?" asks St Peter.

"Oh, I was a consulting actuary," replied the actuary.

St. Peter finds his file and says, "Ah yes, we've been awaiting your arrival as your allotted time on earth has been reached."

The consulting actuary says, "I don't get it. How is that possible, as I'm only 36 years old?"

St Peter looks at the file again and says,

"Well, that can't be right. Based on the number of hours you've billed your clients, you must be at least 98 years old!"

A doctor and a consulting actuary were attending a cocktail party when the doctor was approached by a man seeking advice on how to treat his ulcer.

The doctor offered some medical advice before turning to the actuary and muttering, "I hate it when people ask me for free advice at parties."

The consulting actuary replied, "I completely agree. It happens to me all the time."

The doctor asked, "How do you deal with it? It feels rude not to answer when someone asks for advice during a social event."

"I simply send them a bill for the time," replied the actuary.

The doctor remarked, "That's downright clever. I shall have to remember that."

After the party, the doctor considered writing a bill to the man who asked her about the ulcer but ultimately forgot about it.

Until she opened her mail the following morning and found a bill for £100 from the actuary for "consultation services rendered."

FINANCE

Every American should have above average income, and my Administration is going to see they get it.

Bill Clinton on campaign trail

It's always an unfair trade when you hit a deer with your car.
As you're out the cost of the insurance deductible,
but nature is only out a buck.

What is the definition of a financial advisor?
Someone who keeps investing your money
until it's all gone.

How did the swimmers start an investment fund?
They pooled their money together.

I collect binary variables.
Someday I'll be a booleanaire.

What groups of fish do derivatives traders prefer?
Black Shoals.[119]

Why is Ireland such an excellent investment?
Because its capital is always Dublin.

---

[119] John Lee. Black-Scholes, gettit?

My dad advised me to invest my money into bonds.

So I bought 100 copies of Goldfinger.

Why did the farmer invest in horses?

She heard it was a stable industry.

I am superb at finances.

All my bills are outstanding.

My father recently invested all his money into a German

sausage company.

It was the wurst decision of his life.

What do you call investing your partner's salary into a

cryptocurrency they despise?

Passive aggressive income.

I've started to invest in stocks.

Chicken, beef and vegetable stocks.

I hope one day to become a bouillonaire.

Recently, I made a sizeable investment in a meat company.

I bought a 30% steak.

Why do investors prefer soup to sandwiches for lunch?

Liquidity preference.[120]

Today, I lost my position as a hedge fund manager. It's not clear to me whether this was due to my work performance or breaking the dress code.

All the boss said was something about my shorts and how they didn't cover.

I thought offering 0% mortgages would cause customers to rush to my bank.

But there was literally no interest.

How can you make a small fortune by investing in Bitcoin?

Begin by investing a large fortune in Bitcoin.

---

[120] John Lee

What is the name given to a woman who sets fire to her mortgage documents?

Bernadette.[121]

What animal helps reduce your risk when trading livestock futures?

A hedgehog.

What do you call a liability with no friends?

A loan.

What type of debt was issued by the British secret agent?

A bond, a James Bond.

Why did the investor think he could sell futures in beer so quickly?

Because it was a liquid asset.[122]

---

[121] Burn a debt, gettit?

[122] John Lee

All this talk of trade wars...

it's just Tariffying.

My friend is a man of honour, courtesy, and chivalry.

However, he detests the stock market.

When I asked why, he said,

"Gentlemen prefer bonds."

Why did the actuary drive a steamroller over the bond return?

To get a flat yield.[123]

A boy asked his Bitcoin-investing mum for £10.00 worth of

Bitcoin currency.

Mum: £9.67? What do you need £10.32 for?

After a successful trade, what did the merchant say?

Good buy.

---

[123] John Lee

Every evening as the sun sets, Superman transfers all of his Bitcoin holdings into a conventional mutual fund. It's how he protects himself from Crypto night.

ACTUARIALLY RUDE JOKES

(Not for the risqué-averse)

Big Data is like teenage sex:
everyone talks about it,
nobody really knows how to do it,
everyone thinks everyone else is
doing it, so everyone claims they
are doing it.

Dan Ariely

What's the most embarrassing thing that can happen to a data scientist?

Premature extrapolation.

What do you call it when you do arithmetic for your own pleasure?

Mathturbation.

I've been supplementing my income by creating erotic spreadsheets.

I'm not happy about doing it, but what can I say? sExcels.

What do you call a person who is aroused by the top line of a spreadsheet?

A header-row sexual.

Did you hear about the maths nerd who specialised in trigonometry?

The only angle he was lacking was secs.

What's it called when a distribution can't get an erection?

Percentile dysfunction.

Having sex is like working with fractions.

It's improper for the bigger one to be on top.

What do you call breasts with both magnitude and direction?

Vector quantitties.

The circle reported the tangent line for sexual harassment.

Apparently, it kept touching her.

Did you hear about the perverted actuary?

Standard deviation just wasn't enough for them.

What do you call a statistical donkey that swings both ways?

A bi-ass.[124]

---

[124] John Lee

Actuaries love numbers so much that they do everything by
numbers – they even do sex by numbers.
However, they don't know anyone who'd remotely be
interested in having sex with them.

What do you call a horny square?
An erectangle.

My wife has become much more amorous since I place a large
bear rug in front of my fireplace. She often pulls me onto the
rug and starts kissing me. I genuinely think it's the rug that
makes her horny.
This must be because of Fur-mat's Lust Theorem.

What do you call a one-sided bar with topless dancers?
A Möbius strip club.

My actuarial tutor came out today.
In front of the class, she declared that she was binomial.

How does a pimp tell his prostitute to collect data?

Tally hoe.

Mathematically speaking, the probability of your conception is a spermutation.

Squares are simply quadrilaterals afflicted with a rectangle dysfunction.

Why are motor insurance premiums so high for lap dancers?

Because of their high risk of being rear-ended.

What do you call a group of boys arguing about calculus?

Math debaters.[125]

Did you hear about the two statisticians who tried to use grant money to pay their bill at a strip club?

They were vindicated when it was explained that they were performing a 'posterior analysis'.

---

[125] John Lee, but probably not original.

What do you call a regular series of payments that
sleep around?
A promiscuity.[126]

---

[126] John Lee

JOKE TROPES

You know, we all became
mathematicians for the same reason
— we were lazy.

Max Rosenlicht

KNOCK, KNOCK JOKES

Knock, knock

*Actuary inside stays silent and absolutely still
until knocking stops* [127]

Knock, knock

Who's there?

Actuary.

What's an actuary?

weeps[128]

Knock, knock

Who's there?

Actuary.

Actuary, who?

Haha! Actuaries would never knock on a random person's
door, you fool. We've actually been trying to reach you about
your car's extended warranty.[129]

---

[127] John Lee

[128] John Lee

[129] Created by @MLBactuary

DOCTOR, DOCTOR JOKES

Doctor, doctor, I feel like a fifth of the man I used to be.

Just relax a bit. You're two tenths.

Doctor, doctor, I'm afraid of the vertical Axis.

Why?

Screams

Doctor, doctor, I feel like I'm only a useless spreadsheet.

Don't cell yourself short.[130]

Doctor, doctor, I feel like an actuary.

Don't worry, if you really were an actuary you wouldn't have any feelings.[131]

Doctor, doctor, I'm afraid of the Horizontal Axis.

Oh, my ex had that problem as well.

Screams

---

[130] John Lee

[131] John Lee

CROSS THE ROAD JOKES

Why did the actuary cross the road?
Because that's what they did last year.

Why did the consulting actuary cross back?
So she could charge the client for travel expenses.

Why did the actuary cross the road?
To get away from the recruiter.[132]

Why did PowerPoint cross the road?
To get to the other slide.

Why did the actuary cross the road?
To bore people on the other side.[133]

---

[132] John Lee

[133] John Lee

Why did the chicken cross the road?

Actuarial study manual: The answer is trivial

and is left as an exercise for the reader.

Why did the actuary cross the road?

Never mind that, the real question is: "Why are they outside

the office in the first place?" [134]

---

[134] John Lee

CHANGE THE LIGHT BULB JOKES

How many actuaries are needed to change a light bulb?

Two.

One to find someone with practical skills
and another to peer review their choice.[135]

How many actuaries are needed to change a light bulb?

Zero, after credibility weighting, we have indications
that the bulb is still lit.

How many numerical analysts are needed to change a light
bulb?

2.9974, after five iterations.

How many actuaries are needed to change a light bulb?

There's insufficient data to reach a firm conclusion.

---

[135] John Lee

How many statisticians are needed to change a light bulb?
(1, 3) with 95% confidence.

How many insurance actuaries are needed to change
a light bulb?
None, the insurance department is not permitting any
modifications to the bulb at this time.

How many actuaries are needed to change a light bulb?
One.
They don't have a sense of humour.

How many stockbrokers are needed take to change a light
bulb?
Two. One to take out the bulb and drop it,
and the other to sell it before it crashes.

How many consulting actuaries are needed to change
a light bulb?
Depends. How much money do you have?[136]

---

[136] John Lee

How many actuaries are needed to change a light bulb?

How many did it take last year? Add a margin.

How many consulting actuaries are needed to change a light
bulb?

Sixteen.

One to collect all the information from the client.

One to fill a flip chart with nonsense.

One to whip the interns to collect the data required.

One to write a report about it

and 12 to bill the work of the 16 people

Of course, the light bulb was never changed.

We only tell you what to do and how to do it,

changing the bulb is not our job.

How many economists are required to change a light bulb?

Seven, plus or minus ten.

How many student actuaries are needed to change a
light bulb?

What the hell's a light bulb? That wasn't on the syllabus!

WALKED INTO A BAR JOKES

An actuary walked in to a bar,
where $\bar{a}$ is an annuity paid continuously.

A distribution walks into a bar.
The bartender asks, "What are you having?"
"Just one moment."

An actuary walks into a bar and hastily apologises,
"So sorry, I thought this was the office."[137]

A mathematician walks into a bar and orders a pint. A second mathematician walks into the same bar and orders half a pint. A third mathematician walks in and orders a quarter of a pint. The bartender looks at the infinite queue of mathematicians and says, "You guys should know your limits!" and pours them two pints.

---

[137] John Lee

An underwriter and an actuary walk into a bar.

"Ouch!" yelled the underwriter.

Based on this new data, the actuary warned, "Watch out!"[138]

Three conspiracy theorists walked into a bar.

Now you can't tell me that's just a coincidence.

$f(x) = 3x + 6$ walks into a bar and asks,

"Got any sarnies?"

The bartender replies, "Sorry, we don't cater for functions."

A pivot table walks into a bar.

The bartender says, "Should I start a new tab?" [139]

A student actuary walks into a bar.

The bartender shouts, "What are you doing here?

You should be at home studying!" [140]

---

[138] Actuaries base their predictions on past events.

[139] Jordan Goldmeier

[140] John Lee

A countably infinite number of Mathematicians walk into a bar. However, they all die due to infinite mass in finite space.

A definite integral walks into a bar and orders
five shots of whiskey.
"Are you certain you can handle that?" the bartender asks.
The definite integral replies, "Yeah, I know my limits."

Two actuaries walked into a bar.
That's it. No joke. Actuaries are boring.

A countably infinite number of mathematicians walk into a bar. "A pint of beer, please," asks the first mathematician. "Half pint for me, please," asks the second. "Quarter pint for me," asks the third...
The bartender interrupts, "I don't serve quarter-beers."
"Sorry?" replies a shocked third mathematician.
"No bar serves quarter-beers. That's just silly!" the bartender retorts.
"Oh, come on," pleads the first mathematician, "Do you have any idea how difficult it is to gather a countably infinite number of typically reclusive mathematicians? Just go with it!"
"There are laws on the drinks I'm allowed to serve.

I wouldn't be able to serve a quarter-pint even if I wanted to."
Mathematician #2 adds, "But that's no problem since you'll
pour us a whole number of pints when we reach the end of
the joke. You see, when you take the sum of a series of terms
that halve each time, you obtain-"
"I know how limits work," interjects the bartender.
"I'm sorry. I didn't expect a bartender would be conversant
with such an advanced mathematical technique."
"Are you joking?" replies the bartender. "Limits are taught in
high school! What sort of mathematician considers limits to
be advanced mathematics?"
Mathematician #1 yells, "HE'S ON TO US!" and with that,
the mathematicians make a quick exit and scatter.

A countably infinite number of mathematicians walk into a
bar. It takes forever.

An actuary walks into a-bar and starts drinking continuously.

René Descartes was relaxing in his local bar. The bartender asked him if he wanted another drink. "I think not," replies Descartes, and promptly vanished in a puff of logic.[141]

A unicorn, a fairy and two actuaries walked into a bar.
The unicorn turned to the fairy and said,
"I can't be part of this joke; nobody is going to believe there were *two* actuaries in a bar."[142]

---

[141] René Descartes was a French philosopher most known for his statement: "I think therefore I am."

[142] Mark Denton

TWO KINDS OF PEOPLE JOKES

There are three kinds of actuaries in the world: those who can count and those that can't.[143]

There are 10 kinds of actuaries in the world: those who understand binary numbers and those who do not.

There are 11 kinds of actuaries in the world: those who can count in binary and those who can't.[144]

There are two kinds of actuaries in the world: those who believe that the world can be divided into two kinds of people, and those who don't.

There are 10 kinds of people in the world: those who understand hexadecimal and the other F.[145]

---

[143] Attributed to Fred Kilbourne.

[144] Attributed to Esko Kivisaari.

[145] John Lee

There are two kinds of actuaries in the world:
those who are able to extrapolate from incomplete data.[146]

There are two kinds of experienced actuaries in the world:
those who confess to having made significant forecasting
errors and those who are liars.

There are two kinds of data in the world: uncensored and.[147]

There are two kinds of people in the world.
Actuaries try and avoid talking to both. [148]

There are two kinds of forecasters in the world:
those who don't know and
those who don't know that they don't know.[149]

---

[146] Attributed to Darrel Chvoy.

[147] John Lee, but probably not original.

[148] John Lee

[149] John Kenneth Galbraith

There are 10 kinds of actuaries in the world:
those who understand binary, those who don't
and those who didn't expect this joke to be in base 3.[150]

There are two kinds of actuaries in the world:
those who are bored with these kinds of jokes and...
You know what? I'm done here.[151]

---

[150] John Lee, but probably not original.

[151] John Lee

THE ENCORE

It's true what they say:
inference is bliss.

RISK RATING

If this book made you laugh, then writing a review on Amazon is the most efficient method of warning your fellow actuaries of the risks they'll be exposed to by reading it.

For comedy books, Amazon uses a humour hazard risk rating model with 5 levels. Where 1 indicates all the comedy of a dry textbook and 5 indicates a heretical level of comedy that will result in immediate disciplinary proceedings against the author.

The following link will take you straight to the book page:

mybook.to/ActuarialJokes

And because it's important to peer review any risk assessment, please ensure that you share this book with an actuarial colleague to ensure accuracy in your rating.

THE ACTUARIAL JOKE SANCTUARY

This book provides a secure location for "funny" actuarial jokes that are simply too dangerous to be allowed to roam free in actuarial offices.

Should you encounter such a joke in the ~~wild~~ dull, then please do not approach it, but contact John at **ActuarialTutorUK@gmail.com** who will ensure that trained professionals are sent to retrieve it without risk to yourself or your colleagues.

Every joke retrieved will undergo a rigorous inspection process to ascertain whether it needs to be housed here away from the public or whether its lack of funniness means it's safe to be released back into the world.

Also, we have reason to believe that several jokes contained within the pages of this book have owners. If you are such an owner (and are prepared to admit to being so publicly) then I'll be happy to tag the joke with your name and give you 24 hours to exit the country before I inform the Profession.

RISK MANAGEMENT CPD

Congratulations! To have made it this far demonstrates your dedication to assessing every risk that this book poses. Your thoroughness is a credit to the Profession.

Given that it would be such a waste of your talents to use them on only one book, can I suggest that you earn some extra CPD hours by applying that same thoroughness to my other comedy books:

Confessions of an Actuarial Tutor

Actuarial Fairy Tales

The Ultimate Actuarial Colouring Book

As a bonus, you could even use your skills on my regular annuity of actuarial/mathematical/Excel memes on my free substack. You'll even get discounts on my future books.

ActuarialTutor.substack.com

Finally, if you're also a Christian, then you may be interested to know that I've also written more than 10 Christian parody and satire books, under the pseudonym John Spencer, including "40 Biblical ways to annoy your spouse", "Not the Parables of Jesus" and "The Coronavirus Bible: A pandemic parody" which has raised over £500 for charity.

ABOUT THE AUTHOR

John was born at a very young age with his umbilical cord wrapped around his neck. At first, it appeared that no lasting damage had been done, but as he grew, it became clear that his sense of humour had been damaged irreparably.

John studied mathematics at Oxford University, where he also trained as a teacher. Despite this, he still refers to himself in the third person. Whilst there, he performed stand-up comedy as part of the Oxford Revue. Making audiences laugh was too easy, so he progressed to greater challenges: making maths interesting and making boring actuaries laugh.

When he's not wrestling with his work-life balance or literally wrestling with his four children, he's wrestling with writing funny words on a page in his cramped study.

John lives with his family near Oxford, England, where daily he wonders how his wife still finds the same jokes funny after more than 25 years of marriage.

THE FINAL JOKE

I appreciate that comedy shows often have an encore and so, based on this data, your actuarial model may predict such an encore here.

Seeing as I don't want to be the guy who tells you that your model sucks, I present to you the 670.5th joke:

How do you keep an actuary in suspense?

....

Printed in Great Britain
by Amazon